SEXUAL ENCOUNTERS

SEXUAL ENCOUNTERS

Pacific Texts
Modern Sexualities

LEE WALLACE

CORNELL UNIVERSITY PRESS

ITHACA AND LONDON

First published 2003 by Cornell University Press
First printing, Cornell Paperbacks, 2003

Printed in the United States of America

Library of Congress Cataloging-in-Publication Data

Wallace, Lee, 1962–
    Sexual encounters : Pacific texts, modern sexualities / Lee Wallace.
        p. cm.
Includes bibliographical references and index.
    ISBN 0-8014-4121-8 (cloth : alk. paper) — ISBN 0-8014-8832-X (pbk. : alk. paper)
    1. Sex customs—Pacific Islands—History—Sources.   2. Europeans—Pacific Islands—Sexual behavior.   3. Europeans—Pacific Islands—Attitudes.   4. Pacific Islanders—Sexual behavior.   5. Heterosexuality—Pacific Islands—History—Sources.   6. Homosexuality—Pacific Islands—History—Sources.   7. Cook, James, 1728–1779—Sexual behavior.   8. Banks, Joseph, Sir, 1743–1820—Sexual behavior.   9. Gauguin, Paul, 1848–1903—Sexual behavior.   10. Pacific Islands—Discovery and exploration.   I. Title.

GN662.W35 2003
306.7'09965—dc21

                                        2002155647

Cloth printing   10 9 8 7 6 5 4 3 2 1
Paperback printing   10 9 8 7 6 5 4 3 2 1

For my brothers, Bevan and Dean

Contents

Figures

Acknowledgments

This book trails debts that go back a long way. It was begun more than ten years ago in the English Department at the University of Auckland under the sway of Alex Calder, whose work on the Pacific remains its model. Its second wind came in 1997 via the Marsden Fund of New Zealand, which awarded a grant for a larger collaborative project on sexual representation in Pacific ethnography involving my colleagues Phyllis Herda and Maureen Molloy. The final rewriting of the manuscript was shaped by the generous interventions of anonymous readers commissioned by Cornell University Press, and I hope they can see here the marks of my gratitude. I thank Annamarie Jagose for keeping me company throughout the writing of this book and for making of that process something more than this, its most tangible outcome.

Chapters 2, 5, and 6 have been substantially revised from earlier articles that appeared elsewhere. A slightly shorter version of chapter 2 was published by Johns Hopkins University Press as "Too Darn Hot: Sexual Contact in the Sandwich Islands on Cook's Third Voyage," *Eighteenth-Century Life* 18 (1994): 232–42. An earlier version of chapter 5 appeared as "Tropical Rearwindow: Gauguin's *Manao Tupapau* and Primitivist Ambivalence," *Genders* 28 (1998), http//www.genders.org. A substantially different version of chapter 6 was published as "*Fa'afafine: Queens of Samoa* and the Elision of Homosexuality," *GLQ: A Journal of Lesbian and Gay Studies* 5, no. 1 (1999): 25–39.

LEE WALLACE

SEXUAL ENCOUNTERS

Introduction

This book questions the gender paradigms that dominate thinking about the sexual trajectory described by European desire as it has informed literary, artistic, and anthropological representation of the Pacific. It revises the received image of the South Seas—current since the voyages of exploration in the eighteenth century—as the site of heterosexual pleasures awakened and released in the vicinity of a female body that is unrestrained by civilization's mantle. Instead, I argue that the more sexually resonant figure inscribed within the representational archive of the Pacific is that of a male body, whose variously indulged and proscribed capacities for sodomitical pleasures more keenly register the incoherencies of cultural difference as they are played out within the scene of colonial encounter.

From the first, imperial expansion in the Pacific has been imagined as sexual event. The Enlightenment reception of Louis Antoine de Bougainville's account of Tahiti inaugurates a long tradition of literary representation and ethnographic scholarship within which the Pacific appears as the domain of unchecked heterosexual gratification such that the paradigmatic Pacific encounter between imperial agent and indigenous Polynesian subject is a sexualized one. So we have learned and learned to lament: Pacific history frequently emphasizes the sexual charge of encounter and has persuasively demonstrated the imperial logic and cultural transformations attendant on sexual contact. Yet if Pacific history is everywhere nuanced by a sense of the sexual consequences borne by indigenous populations on European entry into the Pacific, it has neglected to pursue the radical effects of sexual discovery on metropolitan culture. The Polynesian sexual practices witnessed by European voyagers, and crucially those that involve sexual pleasures between men, were the subject of an intense and sustained scrutiny throughout the years of Pacific expansion and colonization. The incorporation of this sexual difference into an ethnographic understanding of the customs of Polynesian culture simultaneously redefined the possibilities for sexual variance within European masculinity. The encounter with Polynesia, and the spectacle of male-male sex, forced the emergence of new terms for thinking about sexual normativity and the capacity for perversion, particularly as it was embodied in masculinity. If we now inhabit those terms fully and unselfconsciously—if, indeed, they define for us the very essence of sexuality—it is worth remembering that they have a particular history, and that history has always been entangled with the representation of the Pacific.

Less concerned with the emergent profile of Polynesian sexual practices than with reading a series of contact encounters and South Seas residencies for their unfolding of European sexual inscription, this book argues that the sexual convergence prompted by the discovery and colonization of the Pacific inevitably entangles with problematics of homosexual definition. In the sexualized discourse of Pacific exploration, colonization, and ethnography, we can therefore trace the counterimplication and historical transformation of both European and Polynesian regimes of sexuality. When considering the practice of cross-cultural sexual observation, this book emphasizes neither the lucidity of interpretation nor its inevitable inadequacy. Rather, it attends to the very opacity of exchange. Between what is said of sexual transactions and what those transactions achieve, a gap appears that measures not the distance between cultural categories but their mutual permeability. The significance of Polynesian sexual practices lies therefore not in their affinity or departure from European models but in the reciprocal evolution of those twin systems. The history of sexual encounter is a history of sexual exchange, whereby each erotic formation implicates the other. European and Polynesian sexual identities are not the same, and neither are they utterly distinct, but what is of continued importance are the changing terms by which they are counterpoised.

Chapter 1 elaborates this argument via an engagement with recent influential theorizations of cross-cultural encounter and gay-inflected historiography and anthropology. Chapter 2 then turns to a historical encounter wherein the sexual conduct of Polynesian men both requires and escapes European definition. This chapter focuses on the documents of Captain James Cook's third Pacific voyage in order to consider the phenomenon of British indifference to Hawaiian sodomitical practices. Of all the early Pacific landfalls, those in the Sandwich Islands were most marked by the fervent solicitation of Europeans by native women. This heterosexual frenzy is much remarked on by the journal keepers aboard the *Resolution* and *Discovery*, whereas they seem less taken up by the evidence of male-male desire among the Hawaiian chiefly class. Their accounts describe the role of the *aikāne* and the political cast given male-male sexual relations, but the observation is almost matter-of-fact. At first glance it appears that the manifestation of this sexual practice cordons the one set of men from the other, keeping Hawaiian and European behaviors distinct. Indeed, when the suggestion is put by the Hawaiians that relations among the British expedition's officers correspond with those between their own chiefs and their male sexual favorites, the British deflect that comparison although the points of similarity nearly outweigh their differences: both sets of relations are hierarchically structured, politically and socially overinvested, and pursued exclusive of feminine demand. The unspoken terms of that rebuttal, I argue, are not that affective alliances between European men bear no relation to power and social advancement. Rather, the relation they do bear is an intensely volatile one, and this volatility is nowhere more apparent than in the institutional regime of shipboard life, where a system of masculine preferment, unmitigated by the presence of women, is sometimes the slick conduit for personal advancement, sometimes its spectacular ruin.

Chapter 3 examines the erotics of male visibility legible across a number of Marquesan contact texts. Beginning with an incident recorded in the texts of the Russian mission to the Pacific of 1803, it considers how, when the spectacle of Marquesan sexual conduct is viewed, the innocence of the imperial viewer is facilitated by the femininity of the native object and an intertextual reliance on prior Pacific documents. Those documents circulate under the authority of a now apotheosized Cook, whose death in Hawaii has been thoroughly woven into the heroic fabric of imperial expansion. Cook's impri-matur licenses, in the far Pacific, a mode of male presence—com-manding, austere, chaste—that is beyond moral reproach. The martyrdom of Cook secured by the Royal Academy, if not the residents of Kealakekua Bay, is indispensable to an imperialist ideology that prefers its watchful masculine agents to be inscrutable. This disembodiment of the European spectator and the sexual immunity it guarantees are, however, confounded when European men find themselves subjected to the voyeuristic regard of the Marquesans. These Marquesan texts, I argue, register two contradictory impulses: the desire to maintain proper imperial protocols around the male body, as evidenced in the invocation of Cook, and the more dubious desire to throw these protocols over, as manifested in the white male beachcomber's embodiment of native practices. The troublesome specularity of the European male is evidenced in both the tattooed body of Jean Baptiste Cabri, a Frenchman the Russians discover living among the natives in the Marquesas, and in *Typee*, Herman Melville's fictional account of his own residence in these islands. In *Typee* the passive American sailor, Tommo, is held captive to other codes of visual appropriation and mastery, and the seaman's errant behavior, which seemingly abandons all codes of imperial conduct, places him in estranging proximity to native men. For both Cabri and his literary avatar, Tommo, the Marquesan residency articulates a more perpetual displacement or exile than that conventionally circumscribed by the romance between itinerant mariner and dusky maiden. In these Marquesan texts the beachcomber figure, who will in later Pacific texts be more thoroughly heterosexualized, is enfolded between two cultures, and his double allegiance reveals not a confidence in the stout separation of sexually distinct codes but a panic at their always imminent collapse.

The suspicion of sodomitical misconduct that clouded the career of William Yate, an early-nineteenth-century New Zealand missionary, is the subject of chapter 4. Beginning with a reading of the documents surrounding Yate's dismissal, I explore the different uses to which the accusation of same-sex contact is put in both the original and more contemporary contexts. The Church Missionary Society's investigation of Yate's sexual encounters with young Maori converts reveals the ideological importance of the rejection of male-male sexual impulse in the legitimization of colonial presence in the Pacific. More than a century later, in the 1970s, the closeted homosexual writer Frank Sargeson was drawn to the subject of Yate's disgrace. Previously understood as nationalist in intent, Sargeson's fiction, and the cult of mateship it is taken to depict, has more recently become embroiled in the interpretative dynamics of homosexual entrapment. Since the posthumous outing of Sargeson, literary criticism, rather than concede the constitutive role homophobia plays in the drawing of national identity, now finds in his laconic men and their often violent disavowal of love between mates the proof of homosexuality. This chapter demonstrates the multiple and often contradictory effects generated around the distinction between the homosexual and the homosocial, arguing that in the colonial discourse peculiar to the Pacific, the elasticity of this distinction provides the means of policing relations among men.

In both its prohibition and its appeal, sodomy remains crucial to this regulatory nexus, and chapter 5 reveals that the bodies of women, as well as men, are drawn into the representational dynamics of male-male desire. This chapter considers Paul Gauguin's *Manao tupapau*, a tropically transversed version of the reclining female figure depicted in Edouard Manet's *Olympia*. Gauguin's painting is interpreted through an incident recorded in his journal, "Noa Noa," a narrative description of the artist's sexual attraction to a native male when he views him from behind on a climb through the forest, in order to demonstrate that the classically sanctioned representation of the female nude plays a part in figuring forth the more illicit possibility of sex between men. The lure of *Manao tupapau* is its display in palimpsestic form of both native fear and European attraction to and anxiety about sodomitical desire. To this end, the painting deploys the Polynesian woman's body, displaying her female corporeality, as a front for male-male sexual interest. Through the representation of an upturned female body, the painting both blinds the viewer to the implication of sodomy and at the same time accesses the perversity associated with that desire.

Chapter 6 analyzes a documentary representation of Samoan male-to-female gender transitivity (*fa'afafine*) and finds in the contemporary television text the pertinence of European sexual description to Polynesian behavior again contested. More than two centuries after Cook opens the Pacific to Western ethnographic description, *Fa'afafine: Queens of Samoa* deploys a now practiced gesture of cultural relativism. The documentary's insistence that Samoan *fa'afafine* are not the same as homosexuals, transvestites, or transsexuals—the Western identity categories they most resemble—is, I argue, best understood as the co-option of an ancient Samoan tradition, so-called, in support of an utterly modern, though disguised, sexual phobia. Under the cover of an alleged liberal tolerance of sexual difference, the narrational strategies of the documentary insist on rendering invisible any suggestion of continuity between Samoan and Western sexual practices, although in relation to patterns of HIV transmission, that denial has dangerous consequences in both Samoa and the sexual subcultures of the Pacific Rim. Concerned with the willful silences that muffle but never stop the circulation of knowledges about same-sex desire, this chapter identifies how the renewed insistence on cultural difference can be used to reinforce a sexual apartheid between Polynesian and European regimes.

In the final chapter I conclude that the discourses of European and Polynesian sexuality stand in heightened relation to the categories of homosexuality and heterosexuality that they help call into existence. Throughout this series of readings *Sexual Encounters* argues that disavowal has been integral to the formulation and dissemination of sexual recognition across Pacific and metropolitan locations since the eighteenth century. That fraught relation between a knowingness and an unknowingness about sexual matters has for so long marked the appearance of homosexual possibility that it now seems hardwired into the circuitry of everyday life. It is, perhaps, worth noting that at least one old Pacific hand warns against trying to see too far into this obscurity, as if the attempt alone would surely implicate the viewer in those hidden proclivities. Describing "the close cribbing" of seamen on a man-of-war, Melville writes of the "contagious" decay that has them in its grip:

> Still more, from this same close confinement—so far as it affects the common soldiers—arise other evils, so direful that they will hardly bear even so much as an allusion. What too many seamen are when ashore is very well known; but what some of them become when completely cut off from shore indulgences can hardly be imagined by landsmen. The sins for which the cities of the plain were overthrown still linger in some of these wooden-walled Gomorrahs of the deep. More than once complaints were made at the mast in the Neversink, from which the deck officer would turn away with loathing, refuse to hear them, and com-

mand the complainant out of sight. There are evils in men-of-war,
which . . . will neither bear representing, nor reading, and will hardly
bear thinking of.

Let the "landsman guardedly remain in his ignorance," concludes
Melville with the full weight of his seaborn knowledge, "and forever
abstain from seeking to draw aside this veil."[1] Such elaborate veiling
is at once an unveiling, and Melville's fulsome description of unspecified "complaints" (as "direful" as they are obscure) enacts the structure of the open secret, the guarding of which fuels the dissemination
of knowledges about which everyone can play dumb. The deck officer,
the landsman, the novelist, and the reader are all drawn into a complicity about the nature of the contagious evil under the cleanly
swabbed decks of the *Neversink*—that it is an evil, that it is contagious. If veiling is the name Melville gives this refusal to do other than
allude and then allude some more, we might clarify that the epistemic
effect of that subtlety is to hold these obscure acts squarely at the fore-
front of thinking and reading and representation, and to keep them
nailed to that masthead as both a knowledge and an ignorance. Same-
sex sexual possibility has held that confused position throughout two
centuries of Pacific representation. In relation to this still growing
archive, it seems warranted to speak not of a Polynesian sexuality or
a Western sexuality but of a shared Pacific sexuality that takes its
shape and volatility from a geographic and discursive field twice
crossed by the histories of homosexual difference and cultural exchange. This Pacific sexuality, from its origins in colonial encounter
to its current reprise in the sexual politics of postcoloniality, continues to be the very paradigm of a modern sexuality.

For this reason, the history of sexual representation in the Pacific is
crucial for rethinking the theoretical and political issues at stake in
gay-inflected reappropriations of the sex and gender regimes of other
cultures. In the chapters that follow I argue that the record of Pacific
encounter reveals not only the historical sedimentation of modern understandings of male homosexuality but also how the distinction between sanctioned and illicit relations between men comes to be

[1] Herman Melville, *White-Jacket*, vol. 5 of *The Writings of Herman Melville*, ed.
Harrison Hayford, Hershel Parker, and G. Thomas Tanselle (Evanston: Northwestern
University Press and the Newberry Library, 1970), 375–76.

regulated and enforced in relation to the new categorical discrimination between homosexual and heterosexual. Male homosexuality,
such as we have come to understand it, was constituted in no small
part through the European collision with Polynesian culture, whose
systems and activities of sexual attraction and desire were so different, or different in such a way, as to throw the European observer into
positions of reaction, denial, or injunction that helped reify modern
categories of sexual identity. Accordingly, my first chapter argues for
the historical entanglement of an ethnographic discourse with the discourse of sexuality, the consequences of which are registered in both
the colonial field and the home precincts of empire.

1 Pacific Texts, Modern Sexualities

> If the Hawaiians really did present their sacred woman to Captain Cook because he was a god, we can be sure he refused her—for something like the same reason.
>
> Marshall Sahlins, *Islands of History*

> But it is Banks who gives us most. He even shows a capacity for going beyond the merely material. He has, in his excitement, his capacity for throwing himself into native ceremonial, his greed for recording everything, become the founder of Pacific ethnography. . . . Most attractive to women Banks certainly was, and—with equal certainty—he carried in his own bosom a susceptible though discriminating heart.
>
> J. C. Beaglehole, *The Endeavour Journal of Joseph Banks, 1768–1771*

This book is concerned with the rhetorical figuring of European masculinity in the record of Pacific discovery and expansion. If James Cook and Joseph Banks can be conceived as the alternative sexual agents of the same project of imperial expansion, they also map between them the outer limits of disciplinary and affective masculinity that such a project allows. The one stands as the model of sexual rectitude, the other of sexual extravagance. Indeed, the figures of Cook and Banks have routinely been used as markers for opposing poles of masculine definition with regard to British adventure in the South Seas. The self-disciplined naval officer and the pleasure-seeking aristocrat who ships with him at his own expense are perhaps flip sides of the same coin. As even the casual reader in Pacific history knows, Banks—who enjoyed the license associated with the English gentleman abroad—willingly immersed himself in indigenous Tahitian ceremonies whereas Cook's Hawaiian venture into cross-cultural mimicry was of deadlier consequence. Banks's celebrated eagerness to engage in Polynesian festivals and to offer his skin to the blemishings of tattoo thus throws into stark relief Cook's inability to do likewise.[1] Similarly, Pacific scholarship has repeatedly wrung from the resolutely secular Cook the sign of the self-made man. In this way the historical contours of an emergent meritocracy can be highlighted by the vestigial privileges granted or assumed by the youthful Banks, the amateur (and seasick) gentleman among career naval officers. If in these accounts Cook is the epitome of British imperial collectedness whose every professional competence indexes that masculinist and nationalist order, Banks seems in danger of losing his nationality and his masculinity altogether. In several of the more popular texts Banks looks decidedly French, particularly in those that circulate rumors of his secreting a cross-dressed female companion in Madeira to accompany him on his proposed second voyage with Cook. Apocryphal perhaps, the story nonetheless recalls Bougainville's time in Tahiti in 1768 when the islanders are said to have disclosed the female identity of one of the French naval officers. Both anecdotes, whether or not they are based in actual incidents, serve as reminders that the peculiar dynamics of Pacific discovery have frequently been associated with unauthorized sexual arrangement and gender crossing.

Banks's long career frequently entangles masculine proprieties in relation to sexual concerns. He can be claimed as the descendant of the tradition of the Grand Tour, in which the education of the aristocracy and sexual errancy went hand in hand, and as signaling the historical eclipse of that masculine rite of passage. As well as foregoing the well-worn geographical route through France, Germany, and Italy, Banks abandoned the itinerary that took in the classical museum alongside the foreign bordello, inaugurating instead the modern ethnographic tour that has as its destination culture itself, as well as the contemplation of its idiosyncratic practices of sex.[2] Whereas sexual initiation

---

[1] For an account of Banks's Tahitian makeover, see *The Endeavour Journal of Joseph Banks, 1768–1771*, ed. J. C. Beaglehole, 2 vols. (Sydney: Trustees of the Public Library of New South Wales in association with Angus and Robertson, 1962), 1:41 and n. 1.

[2] Banks's reply to those that advised he stick to the course dictated by the traditional Grand Tour compresses familiar imperial ambitions even as it redescribes the path those ambitions will take: "Every blockhead does that, my Grand Tour shall be

was an almost compulsory aspect of the Grand Tour, the protodiscourses of ethnography that Banks's Pacific journals record were less decisive with regard to participant observation in matters of sex. Banks did not hold back from such experimentation in the newly opened Pacific, but the effects of that sensuous immersion are less easily recuperable to the discourses of masculine improvement than the sexual circumspection exercised by Cook. However, as Beaglehole's description makes clear, Banks's sexual relations with Polynesian women are most easily validated when given a sentimental cast.

As Mary Louise Pratt has argued, scientific and sentimental discourses came together in the expansionist project of the Enlightenment to enable a new domestic subject for an imperial project that knows no bounds. Banks appears to be auditioning for this domestic role in Beaglehole's account, where his energetic combining of botanical and social pursuits among the Tahitians makes him "the founder of Pacific ethnography." With his "susceptible though discriminating heart" and "capacity for going beyond the merely material," Banks captures the essence of the sentimental agent of imperialism. Compared with his cold-blooded counterpart, whose prototype might well have been the coolly distant Cook, this palpitating male type is, Pratt writes, "positioned at the centre of a discursive field rather than on the periphery." While never holding himself back, this sentimental figure, "composed of a whole body rather than a disembodied eye," is nonetheless "constructed as a non-interventionist European presence" to whom "things happen." "As a textual construct," she argues, "his innocence lies less in self-effacement than in submissiveness and vulnerability, or the *display* of self-effacement."[3] Pratt's conceptualization of a modern imperial ideology of anticonquest, marked by nonheroic narratives of scientific achievement and sentimental immersion, seems particularly applicable to the Pacific voyages of discovery, wherein the concern with the control of territory and colonization of indigenous populations is frequently muted or disguised beneath the production of incremental knowledges, navigational and botanical, that seemingly hold imperial interest at arm's length.

---

one round the whole globe." Quoted in Bernard Smith, *European Vision and the South Pacific, 1768–1850* (Oxford: Oxford University Press, 1960), 14.

[3] Mary Louise Pratt, *Imperial Eyes: Travel Writing and Transculturation* (London: Routledge, 1992), 78.

Representationally shackled to Cook, Banks's masculine affect, his sympathy for and susceptibility to Polynesian femininity, rhetorically mitigates the aggression of encounter and so legitimates European presence in the Pacific. On the *Endeavour,* for instance, although Cook takes his orders from the Admiralty, his voyage is also sponsored by the Royal Society, which provides him and his fellow officers with "Hints" to guide their interactions with native peoples.[4] Insofar as these statements of advice attest to the common humanity of European and native, and impress upon their reader the claims of native title, they are, as Dennis Porter points out, in potential contradiction with the naval instructions that require Cook to cultivate a tactical alliance with encountered populations through no more than the extension of the forms of "Civility and Regard."[5] Cook's journals bear the trace of this contradiction, particularly in those entries that must justify the use of armed force against peoples innocent of European weaponry, but Banks, as the Royal Society's representative on the voyage, is less bound by naval protocol. Free to indulge a sentimental license denied the expedition's commander, Banks is warranted by an Enlightenment ideology that appears to regret or disavow the advances made by the power it serves even as it furthers them.

Together, then, Cook and Banks operate as the tough and soft cops necessary for a successful expedition. In isolation, however, without the symbolic counterbalance provided by Cook, Banks's manliness all but drains away. In both Patrick O'Brian's and Harold B. Carter's biographies, the gendered narrative of Banks's life is a perpetually crossed one wherein the public honors and recognitions afforded him by that elite institution of male clubbability and knowledge, the Royal Society, are offset by his domestic engulfment in a household of women and his running to fat, as if the one phenomenon of enlargement diminished the other.[6] O'Brian goes so far as to include in stones and pounds the—admittedly considerable—weight gains experienced by Banks, his wife, and sister once they took a house together follow-

---

[4] See *The Journals of Captain James Cook on His Voyages of Discovery,* vol. 1: *The Voyage of the Endeavour, 1768–1771,* ed. J. C. Beaglehole (London: Cambridge University Press for the Hakluyt Society, 1967), xcclxxix–xxxiv and 514–19.

[5] See Dennis Porter, *Haunted Journeys: Desire and Transgression in European Travel Writing* (Princeton: Princeton University Press, 1991), 109–10.

[6] Patrick O'Brian, *Joseph Banks: A Life* (London: Collins Harvill, 1987), and Harold B. Carter, *Sir Joseph Banks, 1743–1820* (London: British Museum, 1988).

ing his marriage as if this were, like his less visible Tahitian tattoo, a bodily index to his immersion in an alien, and here feminine, culture. As both slim youth and blubbery spouse, Banks is a test case for how far toward its others masculinity can go. It is as if the sexual example of Banks requires in ballast the alternate example of the self-disciplined Cook if British masculinity is to keep an even keel.

Between them, Cook and Banks provide the coordinates for all subsequent stagings of European masculinity in the Pacific. And if at first these two figures seem to corner the market on masculinity, the Pacific is the location in which the known limits of that masculinity come undone. The poised propriety of the masculine alternatives represented by Cook and Banks is most under threat when the spectacle of male–male sex unfolds, as it frequently did in early Pacific encounter:

> On my Visit this Morning to Tynah and his Wife, I found with her a person, who altho I was certain was a Man, had great marks of effeminacy about him and created in me certain notions which I wished to find out if there were any foundations for. On asking Iddeeah who he was, she without any hesitation told me he was a friend of hers, and of a class of people common in Otaheite called Mahoo [*māhū*]. That the Men had frequent connections with him and that he lived, observed the same ceremonies, and eat as the Women did. The Effeminacy of this persons speech induced me to think he had suffered castration, and that other unnatural and shocking things were done by him, and particularly as I had myself some Idea that it was common in this sea. I was however mistaken in all my conjectures except that things equally disgusting were committed. Determined as I was either to clear these people of such crimes being committed among them, or to prove that they were so, I requested Tynah to inform me, which as soon as I had requested it, a dozen people and even the Person himself answered all my questions without reserve, and gave me this Account of the Mahoos.[7]

The scene is Tahiti in 1789; the observer is William Bligh. Bligh's investigation into Tahitian male–male sexual practice can be claimed as a paradigmatic moment in the South Sea archive, at least as paradigmatic, I argue, as the heavily favored scene in which Polynesian

____

[7] William Bligh, *The Log of the Bounty*, ed. Owen Rutter, 2 vols. (London: Golden Cockerel Press, 1937), 2:16–17.

women make themselves sexually available to European officers and seamen. In this moment the observer of sexual behavior is obscurely implicated in what he sees. At the sight of the *māhū*, "certain notions" open up inside Bligh, which suggest that his familiarity with the Pacific has already triggered speculation about these individuals and their bodily capacities. It is these speculations his interrogation is designed to end, and yet, rather than turn up incontestable proof of Tahitian innocence or guilt of sodomy, thus closing his inquiry, Bligh uncovers a body whose sexual valence exceeds his jurisdiction:

> These people, says Tynah, are particularly selected when Boys and kept with the Women solely for the carnesses [*sic*] of the men, here the Young Man took his Hahow or Mantle off which he had about him to show me the connection. He had the appearance of a Woman, his Yard & Testicles being so drawn in under him, having the Art from custom of keeping them in this position; those who are connected with him have their beastly pleasures gratified between his thighs, but are no farther Sodomites as they all positively deny the Crime. On examining his privacies I found them both very small and the Testicles remarkably so, being not larger than a boys of 5 or 6 Years Old, and very soft as if in a State of decay or a total incapacity of being larger, so that in either case he appeared to me [as] effectually a Eunuch as if his stones were away. The Women treat him as one of their Sex, and he observed every restriction that they do, and is equally respected and esteemed.[8]

Bligh gains an almost shocking intimacy with this transgressive body, whose masculinity can never finally be erased, howsoever small and ineffectual its "privacies" are said to be. Never known for his verbal circumspection, Bligh's salty reportage reveals a fascination with this possibility at least as strong as his avowed disgust, and yet, to point this out is to displace onto Bligh the burden of the sexual inquiry and to make him its convenient scapegoat. Bligh's sharpened interest in the possibility of sexual relations between men, and the precise manner in which they are pursued, indeed prefigures his own later and continually problematic imbrication in the disciplining of masculine pleasures. More important, however, his intrusive examinations take their place among other observations of indigenous sexual regimes

---

[8] Bligh, *Log of the Bounty*, 2:17. The second set of square brackets is the editor's.

which simultaneously redefine the categories available for specifying European male perversity. In being so readily implicated in the act of sexual inquiry, Bligh fails to stand clear of Polynesian sexual difference. Unlike the excited yet decorous representations of heterosexual contact that head so many accounts of Pacific discovery, here it is as if Bligh blunders on indelicately, and yet this indelicacy has less to do with him than with the volatility of representations of male-male desire.[9]

If Cook and Banks are oppositionally defined in relation to their refusal or acceptance of heterosexual offers, the much more ambiguous sexual opportunity figured by the *māhū* cannot so easily be annexed to the professional or sentimental self-definitions of a European masculinity. These newly discovered behaviors—"common" to the Polynesian, according to Bligh, and everywhere observed "in this sea" —are forcefully embedding themselves in the European imagination. Unlike the participants in heterosexual encounters, Bligh can neither reject nor consent to the sexual possibility represented by the *māhū*. Rather, the very existence of such a sexual phenomenon calls forth a new proto-ethnographic discourse that defers to customary practice and at the same time reworks the known codes of masculine conduct. The sexual practices figured by the Tahitian *māhū* announce sexual possibilities between men that cannot be recuperated to extant Euro-

[9] My argument is related, therefore, to that which both Rod Edmond and Vanessa Smith articulate in relation to the missionary William Ellis's account of Tahitian Arioi sexuality in *Polynesian Researches* (1829). Edmond identifies the expediency of the "trope of preterition—the figure by which attention is drawn to something while professing to omit it—to which *Polynesian Researches* often resorts when faced with the untranslatable." Edmond, "Translating Cultures: William Ellis and Missionary Writing," in *Science and Exploration in the Pacific: European Voyages to the Southern Oceans in the Eighteenth Century*, ed. Margarette Lincoln (Woodbridge, Suffolk: Boydell Press in association with the National Maritime Museum, 1998), 158. Where Edmond gives the name *homosexuality* to these "unspecified practices," Smith stops short of such definitional certainty, arguing that Ellis's "persistent oblique references to the moral crimes" of the Arioi are the point at which "the carefully maintained tension between the voices of missionary and ethnographer, destroyer and preserver of traditional Tahitian practices, breaks down. The missionary declares his allegiances: demonstratively balking at an act of description, while producing a site of resonant unutterability in an otherwise discursive text." See Smith's introduction to "Unutterable Practices," an excerpt from Ellis's *Polynesian Researches*, in *Exploration and Exchange: A South Seas Anthology, 1680–1900*, ed. Jonathan Lamb, Vanessa Smith, and Nicholas Thomas (Chicago: University of Chicago Press, 2000), 207. As Bligh is to Ellis in these matters, so is Edmond to Smith.

pean models for thinking about male sexual "crimes." In particular, the older category of sodomy that Bligh invokes in his description is of little use to him in the face of the example of *māhū*. Sodomy defines itself against sanctioned sexual relations, but the *māhū*, who is sanctioned by custom, maps out the more precarious field of sexual normativity across which Polynesian practice and European identity come together and swerve apart. What is traceable in these paradigmatic Pacific encounters is the entangling of nascent categories of modern sexual identity and the ethnographic understanding of Polynesian difference on which those categories hinge.

The Sexual Opening of the Pacific

As will become clear, the space between metropole and periphery is less than stable when codes of masculine sexual conduct are implicated in the revelations of cross-cultural encounter. The eighteenth-century voyages of discovery that opened the Pacific to European navigation exemplify a peculiarly Enlightenment moment in which imperial interest is indistinguishable from the advancement of knowledge itself. Thus, inquiries such as Bligh makes into the sexual behavior of Tahitian *māhū* are not incidental to imperialism but necessary to its facile operation. Imperial discourse, however, does not go unchanged in such moments but is reinflected by the sexual difference it must incorporate within its authoritative classificatory systems. Neither radical nor conservative, the incorporation of this sexually dystopic Pacific into Enlightenment discourse generates far-reaching adjustments in European understandings of sexual possibility and aim. Far more than the heterosexual utopia we are familiar with, the genuine imaginative legacy of European representation of the Pacific is this defining of same-sex sexual desire.

When the *Endeavour* crosses the Pacific, the instructions under which it sails, both military and lay, compel the members of the expedition to observe and record the manners and societal forms of the inhabitants of the lands they come upon. What is of particular interest in this and later voyages, and the travel writing to which they gave rise, is the way in which that chill naval scrutiny and the ostensibly warmer discourses of natural history, as they are applied and extended across the Pacific field, spawn a fledgling ethnography that must, in accordance with the ideology of the Enlightenment, incorporate a knowledge of Pacific sexual behavior into a systematized form of rational understanding. Denis Diderot's popular *Supplément au Voyage de Bougainville* is the most famous of such attempts. Distant in space and time from the Paris in which he writes, Diderot's Tahiti appears on civilization's furthermost horizon as a lost state of nature destined, in the wake of discovery, to be lost yet again. Momentarily, Tahiti represents a place in which, Diderot imagines, nature's order is pleasurably indulged, creating a natural fecundity that fully supports his Enlightenment ideals of profitable increase. His description of connubial relations in Tahiti, including the Tahitian recourse to infanticide and polyandrous or incestuous arrangement, suggests that reproductive utility is unproblematically lodged within a female body whose pleasures and sacrifices serve the social requirements of good natural economy. It is the generative not copulative aspect of Tahitian sexual relations that is emphasized by one of his speakers: "The Venus of Athens and that of Tahiti have next to nothing in common. One is *Vénus galante,* the other *Vénus féconde.* A Tahitian woman one day said to another woman from her country, 'You are pretty; but you bear ugly children. I am ugly, but my children are beautiful, and the men prefer me.'"[10] But if the *Supplément* defines the Pacific as the safe distance at which feminine sexual difference can be known and rationally understood in order to reveal, if not remedy, the sterility, corruption, and hypocrisy of European social organization, it is striking that Diderot's version of Tahiti, like Bougainville's, makes no mention of the Tahitian practices of male-male sexual exchange related by other Pacific voyagers.[11] This occlusion, I argue, maintains European sexual certainty just as later ethnographic reference to such same-sex acts necessarily refigures the European sexual regime.

The erotics of European interest in the Pacific have traditionally been thought of and critiqued in terms of desires adequate to heterosexual mapping, whereby sexual power is located without ambivalence in a masculinity to which femininity is presumed vulnerable.

---

[10] "The *Supplément au Voyage de Bougainville,*" in Denis Diderot, *Political Writings,* trans. and ed. John Hope Mason and Robert Wokler (Cambridge: Cambridge University Press, 1992), 56.

[11] See Robert I. Levy, *Tahitians: Mind and Experience in the Society Islands* (Chicago: University of Chicago Press, 1973), 130–32, for a survey of early accounts of such practices.

Bougainville's account of his ship's arrival in Tahiti in 1768 is perhaps the most idealized staging of this gendered encounter, where, from the dry vantage point of a deck, European vision, at no risk to itself, regards a native femininity seemingly on offer:

> The [canoes] were full of females; who, for agreeable features, are not inferior to most European women; and who in point of beauty of the body might, with much reason, vie with them all. Most of these fair females were naked; for the men and the old women that accompanied them, had stripped them of the garments which they generally dress themselves in. The glances which they gave us from their [canoes], seemed to discover some degree of uneasiness, notwithstanding the innocent manner in which they were given; perhaps, because nature has every where embellished their sex with a natural timidity; or because even in those countries, where the ease of the golden age is still in use, women seem least to desire what they most wish for. The men, who were more plain, or rather more free, soon explained their meaning very clearly. They pressed us to choose a woman, and to come on shore with her; and their gestures, which were nothing less than equivocal, denoted in what manner we should form an acquaintance with her.[12]

Philibert Commerson, Bougainville's naturalist, attributes to the Tahitians a state of nature that is commensurate with heterosexual exclusivity: "The only god they know is the god of Love. Every day is devoted to his worship, the whole island is his temple, all the women are his altar, all the men his sacrificial priests."[13] Though subsequent understandings of the politics of sexual contact dispute the originary innocence claimed by the French navigator in 1771, the heterosexual cast given the narrative of encounter remains almost unchanged, even in the hands of Bougainville's most subtle critics. For instance, whereas Porter's discussion of Enlightenment accounts of circumnavigation articulates the inevitable displacements and deferrals that undermine the imperial logics of travel writing from within, when he turns to Bougainville's observation of Tahitian carnality he writes, "Thus does an eighteenth-century European male 'look,' fix and in-

---

[12] Louis de Bougainville, *A Voyage around the World*, trans. John [Johann] Reinhold Forster (London: J. Nouse and T. Davies, 1772), 217–18.

[13] Philibert Commerson, quoted in Porter, *Haunted Journeys*, 97–98 n. 16. The translation is Porter's own.

terpret the behaviour of alien women of colour," as if no equivalent
ambiguity could be said to unsettle imperialism's sexual optic.[14] Under the banner of a heterosexual assumption Porter must be said to
share with Bougainville and Commerson, the regrettable hierarchies
of gender are brought quickly and unprotestingly into line with those
of racial and cultural difference so that, although he elsewhere decon-
structs the enunciative modalities of imperial acquisition, he permits
sexual colonization to stand as their unambivalent metaphor. More
startlingly, Peter Brooks, in his otherwise nuanced discussion of Paul
Gauguin's primitivism, recalls Bougainville's account of arrival in
Tahiti to invoke not the ground zero of conquest but a sexual sublime
as resolutely heterosexual as it is unremarked.[15]

It should come as no surprise that although many recent studies of
Pacific contact and its representation have challenged any tendency
to oversimplification in fatal-impact versions of Pacific history, stress-
ing instead the adaptable resilience of Pacific culture to missionary
conversion and the more secular inroads of capitalism, no equivalent
revision has shaken contemporary understanding of the sexual politics of imperialism. For example, Bernard Smith's monumental studies of the artistic record left by European navigation of the Pacific,
though finely tuned to the proto-primitivist ideologies that underpin
European aesthetics, do not consider the eroticism of these images as
other than a confirmation of an unspoken heterosexual warrant.[16]
This heterosexual presumption effectively forecloses questions of sexuality, enabling desire to be understood as a unidirectional and un-
problematic force that knits its male and female subjects into stable
if inequitable relation. Thus, even as it foregrounds the gendered nature of the colonial transaction, revisionist history continues to regard
both gender and sexuality as supplements to rather than constitutive
components of the imperial ideologies under analysis. One of the most
far-reaching consequences of this blindness to the hybridized structure of sexual contact and sexual colonization is its failure to recognize the disruptive force of Polynesian sexuality within European
discourse.

[14] Porter, *Haunted Journeys*, 98.
[15] Peter Brooks, "Gauguin's Tahitian Body," *Yale Journal of Criticism* 3, no. 2
(1990): 51–89.
[16] Bernard Smith, *European Vision*, and *Imagining the Pacific: In the Wake of
Cook's Voyages* (Melbourne: Melbourne University Press, 1992).

The erotics of Pacific encounter continue to be understood as involving only their subaltern subjects (inevitably female) not their imperial agents (inevitably male) in historical change. I do not deny that the colonial project was often furthered by men at the expense of women, but I insist that the imperial imagination is gendered in ways that are more complicated than these scenarios first admit. Although recent feminist critiques of the sexual discourses of imperialism have demonstrated that gender itself is transformed in the colonial situation, and that the male–female sexual transactions that are part of the improvisatory repertoire of cross-cultural contact test and revise the uniformity of European self-description, these accounts still betray a residual heterosexism not easily thrown off. While making a forceful argument for the interconnection between the histories of sexuality and imperialism, Ann Laura Stoler contends that colonial technologies for arousing and directing sexual desire for imperial ends anticipate the forms developed for disciplining sexuality in modern Europe. Reflecting on the heterosexual emphasis registered in her own study of the Dutch colonial archive, Stoler refers to the "absent presence of the dangers of homosexuality" in debates about colonial conduct in which "the threat of homosexual desire among stolid Dutch agents of empire, of the colonial *middenstand*, is rarely if ever mentioned. When homosexuality is broached, it is always in the form of a *deflected* discourse, one about sodomising Chinese plantation coolies, about degenerate subaltern European soldiers, never about respectable Dutch men."[17] Uncharacteristically, Stoler appears to take this deflected discourse at its word, accepting that the Dutch record instills an uncrossable discursive barrier between the sexual practices of colonial subjects and those of their colonial rulers insofar as these practices might occur between members of the same sex. Although I am unfamiliar with the Dutch colonial situation, the policing of sexual behavior in the Pacific field is firmly anchored to the notion of, and potential for, homosexual deviancy among the agents of colonization so that the Pacific experience will prove indispensable to the consolidation of metropolitan sexuality and normative understandings of homosexual identity.

My argument marks therefore a discursive shift from both mas-

[17] Ann Laura Stoler, *Race and the Education of Desire: Foucault's* History of Sexuality *and the Colonial Order of Things* (Durham: Duke University Press, 1995), 129.

culinist and feminist studies of the sexual culture of imperialism. I make the case that the record of Pacific encounter reveals that it is the body of the European male, not that of the native female, that incites most interpretative anxiety. In the Pacific it is the civil male body that must define itself in relation to other male bodies, those of Polynesian men, which frequently demonstrate capacities for pleasure that are not easily assimilable to European codes of masculine conduct. The possibility of same-sex relations makes itself felt obscurely throughout the Pacific archives, appearing obliquely within ostensibly straight narratives of contact. The elusiveness of male-male erotics in Pacific narratives indexes the equivocations and denials that are frequently enacted in desire's name. This understanding of sexual impulse restores to desire its full force, as well as its necessarily difficult relation to representation, which in turn might lever open newly complicated understandings of heterosexual contact as well.

The Sexual Politics of Discovery: The New World

Attending to same-sex possibility can inaugurate new and productive understandings of the politics of cross-gender exchange beyond the moment of Pacific encounter. After all, the sexualization of imperial power is by no means confined to accounts of Pacific colonization. Anne McClintock, for instance, detects a similar metaphorizing impulse in no less a critic than Edward Said, whose *Orientalism* insists on the centrality of sexual subjugation to the West's imperial project.[18] Far from rigorously exploring the dynamics of gender as they inform all aspects of Orientalist appropriation, McClintock argues, Said's "Orientalism takes perverse shape as a 'male power fantasy' that sexualizes a feminized Orient for Western power and possession." This sexualized (and—important for my argument—heterosexualized) trope "comes close," McClintock maintains, "to being no more than a metaphor for other, more important (that is, male) dynamics played out in what Said calls 'an exclusively male province.'" Though sexuality is frequently deployed as a trope within imperialist discourse, figuring forth relations to the "virgin" land, for instance, Mc-

[18] Edward Said, *Orientalism: Western Representations of the Orient* (London: Routledge, 1978).

Clintock points out that to continue to deploy it as a metaphor "runs the risk of eliding *gender* as a constitutive dynamic of imperial and anti-imperial power."[19] The representational practices that enfold cross-cultural encounter have received much critical attention in the twenty-five years since Said first stressed the intimacy between forms of knowledge that take as their object other cultures and the history of colonialism and imperialism, but the tendency to heterosexual metaphorization continues. Indeed, if one of the lessons consolidated in the wake of Said's aegis-shifting work is the recognition that the documents of discovery comprise a narrative that bears unreliable relation to the dislocation and violence frequently precipitated by cross-cultural contact, this lesson seems all but forgotten in relation to accounts of sexual conquest that are, almost without exception, taken at their word.

Consider, for instance, the recent literature on the conquest of the Americas in which the Old World's encounter with the New, like the unfolding of the Orient, is a representational act the aesthetics of which can be appropriated for analysis. Following Said's emphasis on representation practices, this critical work has expanded our sense of both the allegorical frame provided discovery by its chroniclers and the incoherence that allegory forestalls. Frequently reproduced and analyzed, Jan ven der Straet's sixteenth-century drawing of Vespucci discovering America is integral to these accounts and is now emblematic of both encounter and its rereadings. Peter Hulme interprets the imperial connotations of the iconic scene as figuring America as a supine temptress whose naked invitation to conquest arouses in the fully armored Vespucci "the masculine thrust of European technology," represented, in this imagining, by the prosthetic devices of flag, sword, and astrolabe.[20] Considering the same illustration, however, McClintock focuses on the diminished female figures who appear in the distance behind and between Vespucci and America, attending a fire above which turns a severed human leg. Dwelling on the literal horizon of the known, these women, she argues, are the "boundary figures" of empire. They mark the "margins of the new world but they

[19] Anne McClintock, *Imperial Leather: Race, Gender, and Sexuality in the Colonial Contest* (New York: Routledge, 1995), 14.

[20] Peter Hulme, "Polytropic Man: Tropes of Sexuality and Mobility in Early Colonial Discourse," in *Europe and Its Others*, 2 vols., ed. Francis Barker, Peter Hulme, Margaret Iverson, and Diana Loxley (Colchester: University of Essex, 1982), 2:18.

do so in such a way as to suggest a profound ambivalence in the European male." Where Vespucci's "erect and magisterial" stature supports a "gaze" that can hold the unclothed America "subservient and vulnerable to his advance," on the periphery of his vision unfolds a cannibal dismemberment that "evokes a disordering of the body so catastrophic as to be fatal." According to McClintock, ven der Straet's drawing represents the "augural scene of discovery" as a "scene of ambivalence, suspended between an imperial megalomania, with its fantasy of unstoppable rapine—and a contradictory fear of engulfment, with its fantasy of dismemberment and emasculation. The scene, like many imperial scenes, is a document both of paranoia and of megalomania."[21] Paranoia and megalomania, it is worth noting, are both heterosexualized in this account.

McClintock's feminized boundary figures, standing at the crossroads of culture, are placeholders for an elemental liminality that oversees the distinctions between "earth-sky; sea-land; male-female; clothed-unclothed; active-passive; vertical-horizontal; raw-cooked" and, we might add, the quick and the dead.[22] These female figures conform to a heterosexual demonology that reaches back to Medusa and forward to her Freudian reworking as the unconscious of encounter. Thus, for McClintock, the denials and fetishistic disavowals attendant on imperial possession are in the service of preserving the tenuous illusion of what is, all the same, heterosexual mastery:

> Suspended between a fantasy of conquest and a dread of engulfment, between rape and emasculation, the scene, so neatly gendered, represents a splitting and displacement of a crisis that is, properly speaking, male. The gendering of America as simultaneously naked and passive *and* riotously violent and cannibalistic represents a doubling within the conqueror, disavowed and displaced onto a feminized scene.[23]

Though insistent that gender is an effect of the colonizing project rather than its precondition, McClintock's analysis, like Hulme's, nonetheless accepts that relations between men and women, or more properly between masculinity and femininity, are candidly emblematic of the ambivalence attendant on fantasies of possession. The ex-

---

[21] McClintock, *Imperial Leather*, 26–27.
[22] McClintock, *Imperial Leather*, 26.
[23] McClintock, *Imperial Leather*, 27.

tent to which McClintock pursues this argument also determines the extent to which she fails to recognize that this heterosexual ideology might be itself produced and naturalized in such moments in a process that is central to the legitimization of imperial power.

If in order for the power relations of empire to be normalized, they must first be heterosexualized, then these accounts might be said to confirm rather than critique the heteronormativity of Vespucci's representation of encounter. Attention, it seems, needs to be given to the representational mechanisms through which the explicit heterosexuality of the imperial relation is secured. In this context Jonathan Goldberg argues that the heterosexualization of New World encounter is achieved by the necessary invocation of its sexual antithesis. Though frequently overlooked by other historians, one of the projects unleashed by the Renaissance discovery of the New World was, according to Goldberg, the "systematic persecution of so-called sodomitical Indians."[24] Thus the process of gendering the New World feminine battens down with a peculiar violence on native men, though that corollary effect often goes unnoticed by criticism that tends to assume—indeed, insists—that their feminization is only metaphorical. In the Spanish texts of discovery, Goldberg traces the deployment of the concept of sodomy to license violent pogroms against the inhabitants of the Americas, acts that take as their precedent Vasco Núñez de Balboa's slaughter in 1513 of forty Quarequa Indians accused of "most abhominable and unnaturall lechery."[25] Confusing gender with their effeminacy and outraging the prerogative of procreative sexuality by their sexual servicing of other men, these forty male bodies have an abusive aspect that works to "infuse Balboa's acts with moral purpose," which is amplified in the aftermath of the execution as the surviving Quarequa deliver to his purifying command more from among themselves "infected with that pestilence."[26] The representation of

[24] Jonathan Goldberg, *Sodometries: Renaissance Texts, Modern Sexualities* (Stanford: Stanford University Press, 1992), 179.

[25] Having defeated and killed the leader of the Quarequa and six hundred of his soldiers, Balboa finds in the house of the slain noble's brother a host of "younge men in womens apparell, smoth & effeminately decked," kept for the pleasure of "preposterus venus." Forty of these cross-dressed minions he orders fed to the Spanish attack dogs. Goldberg is citing the 1555 English translation of Peter Martyr's *Decades. Sodometries*, 180.

[26] Goldberg, *Sodometries*, 181; Martyr, *Decades*, quoted in Goldberg, *Sodometries*, 182.

sodomy, Goldberg argues, serves to divide the native population into noble and ignoble savages, allowing the Spanish conquest to be framed as an exemplary action, a liberatory intervention made at the request of those who suffer because of the "stinkynge abhomination" practiced by their corrupt leaders.[27] The bodies of these effeminate men are thus "a locus of identity and difference, a site for crossings between Spaniards and Indians, and for divisions between and among them."[28]

This invocation of certain sexual practices as proper or natural claimants to space against other, unnatural practices that must be expelled by any means is crucial to the story of conquest. The representation of sexuality operates in excess of the requirements of narrative, supplying "ideological justifications that are elsewhere lacking in the account."[29] It is as though it were insufficient for the Spaniards to win the day martially: Balboa's expeditionary force still requires the expulsion of difference—and a difference of this kind, with its appeal to divine sanction and also to the will of those oppressed by its indulgence—to establish its license and its urgency, to justify both European occupancy and the violence on which it depends. The colonial annexation of new territories in the Americas will hereafter have its legitimacy supported by the eradication of perverse practices attributed to its indigenous peoples, an eradication that is nevertheless carried out on their behalf.

The example of the New World reveals the relation of heterosexual metaphorization to the justification of the power relations of empire. Sodomy acts as the rhetorical category elastic enough to invoke and legitimately repress indigenous peoples. However, this rhetorical category is no longer available to the rationalist discourses of the Enlightenment, which, once they venture into the Pacific, must explain, not simply judge, the spectacle of male–male sexual relations. Relative to prior ideologies of conquest, the later epoch of imperialism cloaks its relation to power behind a secular and apparently "benign" natural history that seeks to incorporate anything and everything—including sexual behavior—into a "rationalising, extractive, dissociative understanding."[30] Such explanation of Polynesian same-sex sexual activity

<hr>

27 Martyr, *Decades*, quoted in Goldberg, *Sodometries*, 182.
28 Goldberg, *Sodometries*, 184.
29 Goldberg, *Sodometries*, 184.
30 Pratt, *Imperial Eyes*, 38.

makes, for the first time in history, reasonable or rational (rather than treasonous or offensive) the parallel possibility of similar relations among European men.

Sodomy and Homophobia

Before we return to the Pacific, there is a pressing need to examine a troubling loop in Goldberg's argument whereby the archaic category of sodomy is linked to a homophobia that makes sense only in the context of contemporary sexual identification. Balboa's massacre of the sodomites is claimed by Goldberg as an "originary moment" in the founding of the Americas in a gesture designed to dislodge from their position of unquestioned preeminence other events (discovery, colonial survival, the granting of political autonomy) more regularly celebrated in the calendar of nationhood ("Columbus Day, Thanksgiving, Independence Day").[31] This is done not simply to add yet another memorial day to an increasingly crowded program but in order to reveal the homophobia that continues to underwrite American (that is, United States) citizenship in the present. This swerve from the past to the contemporary occurs twice in Goldberg's discussion, and it is the second, less polemical of these moments that raises problems of methodology that have consequences for my own argument. Having identified these "complicities" between the colonial project and the representation of the sodomitical body, Goldberg goes on to suggest that the seal between the two is less than watertight.[32] Produced as a site of both difference and identification, the sodomitical body features within colonial texts "as the body that needs to be effaced" but also marks "an ineffaceable site of disruption."[33] Like McClintock's female boundary keepers, Goldberg's native sodomite is the embodiment of a representational double bind whereby colonialist allegory produces the New World as the site of imitation as well as departure, but in being simultaneously doubled and displaced by the mirror of America, the European original suffers a declension that cannot be recuperated.

---

[31] Goldberg, *Sodometries*, 179.
[32] Goldberg, *Sodometries*, 186.
[33] Goldberg, *Sodometries*, 187.

Somewhat problematically, however, the radical alterity that Goldberg locates in the sodomitical body, its capacity to corrode the representational certainties of an Old World order, is, it seems, recoverable under the term "indigenous homosexuality."[34] Swerving from the Renaissance to the modern via an excursion on the "ordinary homophobia" that underwrites twentieth-century anthropological interpretation of sexual diversity among Native Americans, Goldberg argues for a retrieval of the Native American's cross-gendered body and its "preposterous truth" that, although never singular in its meanings, nonetheless adequately stands for "a cross-identification that could define men's bodies or women's bodies, and the multiple possibilities for sexual relations of men with men, and of women with women."[35] *Sodometries* contends that those same-sex possibilities were murderously forfeited in the Spanish invasion of the New World and the later colonization of New England, where the figure of the sodomite is invoked to discipline and regulate the Puritan brethren themselves, to establish where the exclusivity of an ideal community begins and ends.[36] Furthermore, Goldberg argues, the erasure or containment of same-sex desire remains central to the contemporary public discourse of sex in the United States.

That the ideological programs of discovery and colonization, like that of more recent national policy, are reliant on sodomy for their legitimation is, indeed, well documented by Goldberg. However, his invocation of an "indigenous homosexuality" in the place of this previously stigmatized category, sodomy (a rhetorical figure for improper or unnatural relations that has no immediate correspondence with those desires and identity formations now organized under the modern terms of sexual orientation), seems less historically grounded. Though honed by the ideological necessities of conquest, Balboa's violent acts are steeped in Christian precept. Evolving from notions of divine sanction and sharpened for more secular requirements, sodomy is available as an a priori moral category both dense and slippery enough to be wielded throughout the contingencies of encounter with spectacular effect. Homosexuality, however, though displaced to a

---

[34] Goldberg, *Sodometries*, 282 n. 15.

[35] Goldberg, *Sodometries*, 282 n. 15, 192–93.

[36] Goldberg, *Sodometries*, 223–46. See also Michael Warner, "New English Sodom," *American Literature* 64, no. 1 (1992): 19–47.

footnote, seems available only belatedly as a rhetorical tool with which to redress or at least reveal history's homophobic impulse. The violence of history is undeniable, but the antihomophobic response it calls up derives, anachronistically, from outside the representational archive itself. Not only is the past placed in the service of a contemporary politics, but so too are native sexual practices; the historical slippage is matched by a second slippage that reclaims a homosexuality now identified as the traditional cultural property of indigenous peoples.

The history of sexual representation in the Pacific can, it seems to me, provide what Goldberg's argument lacks: a context for thinking about the historical evolution of homophobia. My own critical project, like Goldberg's, is oriented toward the sexual alterity that is to be heard in the record of cross-cultural contact, not to lament its loss in the violence of encounter or to retrieve it within other representational ethnographies (say, a less homophobic anthropology), but to listen for the differences momentarily released in contact that will then harden into new categories for understanding sexual possibility. Goldberg argues—anachronistically—that the heterosexual legitimation of discovery is fueled by a virulent homophobia, but there is more to be gained by refusing to call any relation between those two forms preemptively. It is not that the sexual discourses of Pacific discovery, as heterosexual as they frequently are, have no relation to modern homosexuality or to homophobia but rather that they produce both categories as their historical effect.

From Sodomy to Homosexuality: The Pacific

Goldberg's analysis of the facility with which the category sodomy is wielded to legitimate imperial violence and appropriation in the New World should redouble our interest in early Pacific travel writing insofar as Pacific expansion is synchronized to the rationalist discourses of the Enlightenment. The texts of Pacific encounter frequently address the spectacle of male-male sexual exchange, but in so doing they redefine sodomy and produce new epistemological categories for specifying sexual behavior. The modernization of sexual understanding that Michel Foucault has taught us to identify as one of the legacies of the Enlightenment was inextricably entangled with the emergence of an ethnographic understanding of other cultures. This connection is nowhere more evident than in the dissemination of proto-ethnographic accounts of, in particular, the male-to-male sexual behavior that European travelers observed on entering the Pacific. Though such practices had traditionally been recognized as sodomy, the moral despicableness of which was transparent, the rise of natural history required that such a phenomenon could no longer be thought innately vicious. The discourse on sexuality thus evolves in tandem with representations of Polynesian cultural difference, and the interconnection of the two is traceable in the reimagining of sodomy not as a prohibited act but as a form of behavior that manifests a difference without and also within European civilization.

In his encyclopedic study of Western sexual ethnography, Rudi C. Bleys argues that the discursive transformation of the Enlightenment required that the native sodomite be reconfigured in the context of a continuum of human nature that extended from the natural to the civil, a requirement that brought the behavior observed abroad into relation with the regulation (and subsequent pathologization) of similar same-sex sex acts known to involve European men. Bleys's study incorporates travel reportage from the Americas, Africa, and Asia, but his thesis is most vividly enacted in the evolution of the Pacific archive of contact precisely because this reportage commences in the late eighteenth century and does not have to be disentangled from earlier constructions of the sodomitical baseness of the Oriental, the Moor, or the savage inhabitant of the New World. Within the Pacific archive a shift can be traced in ethnographic accounts of Polynesian male same-sex behavior which has a parallel in the solidifying discourses of modern sexology. Whereas at the beginning of the period of Pacific expansion journal keepers note an array of male-to-male sexual alignments that correspond to various differentials of age and rank, by the moment of the missionary William Ellis's *Polynesian Researches* (1829) male same-sex sex practices are understood exclusively in relation to a gender distinction wherein one male partner assumes a feminine role.[37] Evidence of cross-gender identification in Tahiti can therefore, argues Bleys, be made to serve the advancement

---

[37] Rudi C. Bleys, *The Geography of Perversion: Male-to-Male Sexual Behavior outside the West and the Ethnographic Imagination, 1750–1918* (New York: New York University Press, 1995). Bleys gives the year of *Polynesian Researches* as 1830.

in Europe of a new understanding of sodomy as the province of a sexual minority that will be known by the end of the nineteenth century as a "third sex." This pattern furthers the Enlightenment's "gender revolution," whereby older moral understandings of sexual protocol are eclipsed by the *"cognitive* definition and classification of sexual desire, based on biological assumptions concerning the normative authority of human nature, and connecting sex and gender to one another in a way that was far more coercive than before."[38]

Bleys goes on to argue that at the end of the nineteenth century ethnographic writing about Polynesian same-sex practices bears a different, though still informing, relation to sexological understandings of perversity that, via the ideological mechanism of racial primitivism, are now linked to an understanding of sexual degeneracy. Thus, late-nineteenth- and early-twentieth-century writings on the Pacific, insofar as they stress the ritualized, age-structured, and transitional nature of sex acts involving Polynesian and Melanesian males, produce a new cultural profile for the sexual subject. In these later ethnographic analyses same-sex sex acts, frequently pederastic, pertain at least potentially to entire male populations rather than specified minorities or the members of a "third sex" and therefore promote a rhetoric of sexual acts rather than sexual identities. Bleys stresses, however, that early-twentieth-century sexology sought to consolidate the Pacific as a region in which such institutionalized homosexuality occurred in order to confirm "its artificially constructed cognitive divide between 'circumstantial' and 'congenital' homosexuality." If the Pacific could be cited as the location in which "'genuine homosexuality' did not occur," a contention upheld by the very ubiquity of Polynesian and Melanesian same-sex activity, then this "supported rather than refuted the validity of sexual taxonomies at the home front."[39]

The point I extrapolate from Bleys is not simply that a primitivist ideology underwrites sexology, just as it will the somewhat later field of psychoanalysis, but that in the discourse of ethnography, sexuality functions as the critical link between culture and race theory, ideologies from which its own genealogy cannot be divorced. The description of Pacific sexual practices, I would add, has no straightforward or uniform relation to modern regimes of sexuality—or to the related dis-

---

[38] Bleys, *Geography of Perversion*, 2.
[39] Bleys, *Geography of Perversion*, 185.

courses of race and culture—and this is apparent precisely when the Pacific archive is said to augur the distinction drawn, if muddily, by late-nineteenth-century discourses of sexuality, namely, the distinction between sexual acts to which anyone is susceptible and the notion of congenital deviancy lodged in a particular personality. Although Bleys's account suggests a series of historical supersessions in which a gender-transitive model of congenital perversity replaces a prior moral model of sodomitical vice, to be in its turn replaced by an environmental account of same-sex activity, the more persuasive point is that between them these different axes of understanding—the gender-liminal and gender-separatist, minoritist and universalizing—define the field on which homosexuality is situated not as a stable or coherent category but as a highly mobile one. Moreover, any one of these defining traits can be emphasized or enabled depending on the requirements of the larger discursive moment. In the sexual regime of modernity the specificity of homosexuality is never settled once and for all, but the contradictory definitions it encompasses can be variously and even simultaneously called up and deployed in order to police other more necessary distinctions, such as that between the sexual behaviors of metropolitan and peripheral subjects.[40]

Contemporary Theorizations of Homosexuality

The crucial historical role played by the observation of Pacific sexual behaviors in setting the terms for understanding and disciplining

[40] It is precisely this issue—the differential disciplining of male sexuality at home and abroad—that fuels Christopher Lane's critique of Ronald Hyam's influential study of the sexual relations enabled by British imperialism. Hyam argues that imperial fields offered, indeed promoted, opportunities for the expression of desires less restricted than those permitted at home, and the peculiar nature of the British colonial establishment, unlike its European counterparts, lay in its incitement of sexual desire, including desire between men, which could then be successfully harnessed to the disciplined practices of military and bureaucratic rule. Thus Hyam is able to argue that same-sex desire, frequently sublimated, was integral to British imperial efforts. Lane takes Hyam to task for the political and no less historical naiveté with which he can ignore that the existence of a cordon sanitaire around colonial homosexuality leaves intact the imperial regime of heterosexual normativity. See Ronald Hyam, *Empire and Sexuality: The British Experience* (Manchester: Manchester University Press, 1990), and Christopher Lane, *The Ruling Passion: British Colonial Rule and the Paradox of Homosexual Desire* (Durham: Duke University Press, 1995).

metropolitan sexualities is not confined to the Enlightenment or to the late-nineteenth-century moment that saw the clinical birth of the homosexual. The Pacific is still integral to transformations in both specialist and nonspecialist understandings of the sexual field, although these transformations are now frequently motivated by the agendas of post-Foucauldian theorizations of homosexual desire and identity. Contemporary debates on the formation of homosexual identities often draw on the Pacific—a portmanteau term taken to include the representation of both Polynesian and Melanesian sexualities—as a definitional crucible for their transcultural and transhistorical arguments. As site of sexual metaphorization, the Pacific is not an anachronistic rhetorical device but a current and volatile discursive space across which shifts in sexual knowledge continue to be registered and contested. Pacific representation, in this sense, continues to drive a wider project of sexualization and can be seen to have had a determining influence in the late-twentieth-century formation of sexuality studies.

The comparative dynamics that operated within the nineteenth- and early-twentieth-century sexological project are replayed one hundred years later in the cross-cultural study of Pacific, particularly Melanesian, homosexualities, which similarly involves discussion of the part of culture in shaping sexual destiny and expression. The conception of ritualized homosexuality, for example, has been utterly reinvigorated in the context of gay-inflected reconsiderations of the social as well as psychic origins of same-sex sexual behavior. In this body of anthropological work the insistence on the normativity of male-male sexual contact in Melanesian cultures indexes, however mutely, the aberrant status those relations are accorded in Western culture. In the 1980s Gilbert Herdt's agenda-setting study of sexual rituals within the Sambian cultures of the New Guinea highlands provided a more general gay criticism with an exemplary account of a masculinist ideology of same-sex conduct wherein proper male development necessarily involved sexual induction between boys and older youths.[41] Among the Sambia, according to Herdt, homosexual relations were not a deviation from the proper course of sexual matura-

---

[41] Gilbert Herdt, *Guardians of the Flutes: Idioms of Masculinity* (Chicago: University of Chicago Press, 1994), and *The Sambia: Ritual and Gender in New Guinea* (New York: Holt, Rinehart and Winston, 1987).

tion but a compulsory aspect of the induction of male youths into an adulthood eventually and exclusively marked as heterosexual. This account of male sexual ritual circulated well beyond the academic field in which it was anchored, bestowing on the Sambia a symbolic status far in excess of their importance to anthropological debate. Often cited in the texts that comprise the foundations of gay studies, the ubiquity and cultural centrality afforded same-sex sexual relations among the Sambia was taken to graphically reveal that homosexual relations had no necessary relation to the aberrant or derogatory status Western culture uniformly bestowed on them. This modern homosexual project, as different as it is from the heterosexual rhapsodizing of the Pacific undertaken by Bougainville and Diderot in the late eighteenth century, is nonetheless continuous with it insofar as the peripheral erotic formation is repeatedly invoked to gain more critical agency for a metropolitan sexual subject.

This gay-political interest in the Sambia now seems somewhat at odds with both Herdt's initial study of age-stratified male-male sexual initiation among New Guinean tribesmen and its subsequent revisitings. While acknowledging that sexual potentialities are always mediated by social conditions (in this case the belief that masculine potency, involving physical strength, social maturity, and reproductive competence, is transferred—diminished and increased—via the exchange of semen), Herdt's account of the manner in which young boys learn to fellate older bachelors in order to obtain and ingest the semen they require to grow into men insists on the erotic aspect of these practices. In so doing, Herdt writes against a long tradition of anthropological investigation of institutionalized homosexuality which reads the sexual activities of tribal members solely as the manifestation of social structures and the enactment of relations of power. In failing to inquire into the subjective experience of the participants in those activities, Herdt maintains, this older anthropology shores up the assumption that sexual identities are the exclusive property of modern metropolitan subjects.[42] Herdt's more recent ethnographic interviews among the Sambia further suspend this mechanistic approach to indigenous sexual acts in order to inquire into their agents'

---

[42] Herdt argues this most forcefully in "Representations of Homosexuality in Traditional Societies: An Essay on Cultural Ontology and Historical Comparison, Parts 1 and 2," *Journal of the History of Sexuality* 1, no. 3 (1991): 481–504; no. 4 (1991): 603–32.

affective and phantasmatic relations to those activities. Herdt's critical gesture, it seems, is one of relativism whereby the investigation of the Sambian experience of the erotic—a category previously assumed to subtend only Western sexual subjects—enables a genuinely cross-cultural analysis of homosexuality.

This comparative gesture, and its homosexual emphasis, has been staunchly criticized, however, by Deborah Elliston, who argues that—however enabling the Sambian study was on first appearance—Herdt's reliance on the erotic defeats the purpose it was designed to achieve. The erotic, she argues, cannot be foundational to the cross-cultural study of homosexuality since it engages Western ideas about sexuality that continue to obscure the indigenous meanings of those practices. How is it, asks Elliston, that the notion of sexuality can still be ethnocentrically presumed in the very practice of a comparative ethnography designed to dislodge it? Elliston persuasively identifies how the gesture of cultural relativism quickly folds back on itself and reanimates those sexual categories it sought to cast aside. Her critical remedy nevertheless suggests the difficulty of escaping the epistemic collapse of relativism. In an attempt to gain some analytical distance from Herdt's work, Elliston suspends the term *homosexuality* and proposes instead a "substance-based" model for thinking about the "semen practices" of three distinct Melanesian societies in order to point up the indigenous meanings that attach to these exchanges and the part they play in the constitution of social identities heavily marked by age and gender hierarchies.[43] In her analysis, that is, the category of gender dislodges that of sexuality.

Margaret Jolly and Lenore Manderson have identified a similar stand-off evident in much classical anthropological work on the Pacific, which tends either to subsume sexuality under gender and reproductive capacity or to import Western psychoanalytic categories of sexual subjectivity that assume desire is sovereign to the individual and innocent of the claims of sociality or history. In the one case, sexuality is eclipsed by gender and an emphasis on the kinship structures that underwrite the latter category and do not recognize the former; in the other, sexual desire and action are reified in an individuated subject of sexuality that derives from a Western model and is unsustained

---

[43] Deborah A. Elliston, "Erotic Anthropology: 'Ritualized Homosexuality' in Melanesia and Beyond," *American Ethnologist* 22 (1995): 848.

by the indigenous sexual regimes of the Pacific.[44] I wish to argue, however, that the anthropological debate between Herdt and Elliston indexes something peculiar to the history of sexuality, and to the particular history of homosexuality as it emerges in Pacific representation. Herdt's gay-resonant anthropology pursues an account of Melanesian cultural practice that is consistent with a modern model of homosexuality that privileges sexuality over gender. It thus places itself in opposition to a tradition of writing about Pacific male-male contact which has frequently raised the claims of gender identification above those of sexual activity. In Pacific anthropology this incoherence is often spatially resolved as each model takes on a geographical specificity, being associated with either Melanesian or Polynesian practices, respectively.[45] Elliston's critical revision forestalls this geographic or spatial solution by insisting that the relation between the male and female categories of gender is the operative distinction for understanding the significance of semen exchange among the New Guinea highlanders.

These divergent anthropological models for understanding the significance and origin of same-sex male behavior—gender-separatist or gender-liminal, minoritizing or universalizing—are the same models that were invoked by a much older sexology when it first incorporated descriptions of Pacific sexual behavior into its disciplinary order. These discrepant models continue to inflect contemporary theorizations of sexuality, producing homosexuality—and the sexualized Pacific—as a space of conceptual incoherence. The gesture of comparativism, which is provoked by the desire to sidestep those contradictory models, can never do so because they originate within that

---

[44] See the compelling introduction to *Sites of Desire, Economies of Pleasure: Sexualities in Asia and the Pacific,* ed. Margaret Jolly and Lenore Manderson (Chicago: University of Chicago Press, 1997), 1–26. The greatest challenge to this orthodoxy has come from recent feminist-inflected studies of gender and colonialism which acknowledge that although sexuality is frequently underpinned by gender, they are not the same thing, nor is either category transparent across culture and time. This body of work has begun to generate an understanding of sexual desire as thoroughly implicated in relations of power that when exacerbated by colonial exchange, mutually transform both the forms of sexual expression and their manifestation in practices of gender.

[45] See the essays collected in *Ritualized Homosexuality in Melanesia,* ed. Gilbert Herdt (Berkeley: University of California Press, 1984), and *Oceanic Homosexualities,* ed. Stephen O. Murray (New York: Garland, 1992).

comparative frame. Considered within the discursive history of Pacific ethnography and modern sexuality, Elliston's engagement of Herdt has the structure of a repetition. Her critique raises the terms of the original debate to the next power, but it cannot disengage from them entirely. The ethnographic impulse toward relativism rather than counterclaiming the metropolitan sexual model serves only as its continued exemplification.

The chapters that follow reconsider the historical entanglement of Western and peripheral sexualities, resetting in consequence both ethnographic and gay-historical agendas. The role of the Pacific in the constitution of the modern notion of the homosexual is, I have said, felt beyond the specialized fields of sexology and ethnography. The readings that comprise this study focus on various documents that record, however obliquely, European men responding to the diverse example of Polynesian masculinity, particularly those moments when European men experience themselves (and particularly their corporeality) as knitted in to some Polynesian order of meaning that is radically opposed to their own social and erotic codes. In these moments the experience of the South Seas produces a sexual counterintelligence that erases the certainty of European self-knowledge so that the hesitancy and vulnerability of encounter is garnered to the male subject, who is a reluctant, though nonetheless efficient, agent of colonial expansion. By the late nineteenth century it is precisely this experience that European visitors such as Gauguin require of the Pacific—that it will sexually undo and remake a man as other than he has been before.

Against the tide of European fantasies of the South Seas as heterosexual utopia, I argue that it is the male body—whether native or European—not the female which provides the sexual vanishing point that structures many Pacific narratives. In each of these Pacific moments a privileged figuration occurs: the body that stands as place-marker for erotic capacities both indulged and forsworn is indicatively male. These inscriptions of masculinity betray a certain amplifying anxiety: the discrepant sexual availabilities recorded in each text break with increasing urgency on the shore of heterosexual and homosexual definition. Even as these Pacific journal keepers, these writers and artists, map identity more and more ferociously onto the known grid of gender, the horizon of sexual certainty seems to recede further and further. Exacerbated by the cross-cultural contact attendant on Pacific expansion and settlement, the discursive conditions emerge through which modern homosexuality can appear. The historical engagement with the island cultures of the empire's periphery—and the sexual possibilities they represent—compels a new definitional order in which the charged opposition between the heterosexual and the homosexual comes to function as the preeminent classificatory distinction through which European culture learns to specify not its Polynesian subjects but its own.

2 Sexual Encounter in Hawaii on Cook's Third Voyage

Captain James Cook's third voyage is paradigmatic of European-Pacific encounter. The importance of this voyage has long been reckoned in terms of the figure of the native woman. Recent postcolonial revisionist narratives, no less than original accounts of the voyage, understand its significance and calculate its implications in terms of a native femininity that accelerates exchange between Hawaiian and European cultures. Though not unimportant, this sexual encounter functions as a blind for a far more complicated because far less articulable relation between men, native and European. Considering the journals of Cook's third voyage, this chapter argues that the male body is troublingly inscribed with the erotic consequences of contact. I am not simply suggesting that by some judicious switch the native man can more properly take the position customarily ceded to the native woman. As my readings demonstrate, I am equally arguing that a focus on the erotic capacities of the male body enables a significant rethinking of the European masculinity that in most versions of encounter, remains untransformed, the neutral measure against which all change is reckoned.

Desire

According to the journal keepers aboard the *Resolution* and *Discovery*, the sexual fervor that met their landfall in the Sandwich

Islands in November 1778 eclipsed expectations whetted even by Tahiti. The motivation behind the Hawaiian women's blatant solicitation of the seamen of Cook's third voyage has been the subject of much interpretation, most of it skewed by a knowledge of the circumstances in which the British ships will finally depart the island of Hawaii, having suffered the loss of their commander at the hands of the residents. As the original British participants in these events recognized, their appearance in these islands from across the seas was interpretable according to the Hawaiian festival calendar. In consecutive years, 1778 and 1779, the comings and goings of the *Resolution* and *Discovery* coincided with the time of Makahiki and the annual enactment of the return of the fertility god Lono. The significance of this misprision of Cook and the Hawaiian god Lono has recently become one of the most contested points in critical anthropology: Gananath Obeyesekere has challenged Marshall Sahlins's structuralist analysis of this cross-cultural recognition in order to assert the intentionalist significance of its fatal outcome.[1] According to Obeyesekere, Sahlins's insistence on the symbolic confusion surrounding the events that led to Cook's slaughter denies native agency in what is better read as an act of resistance against an alien power that is everywhere recognized for what it is, not what it resembles. Rod Edmond, in a deft and elegant commentary on this "gladiatorial" stand-off, draws attention to the way "each antagonist, in effect, tries to cast the other as Cook. Sahlins becomes the proto-imperialist that Obeyesekere takes Cook to have been; Obeyesekere becomes the European realist that Sahlins assumes Cook was. The death of Cook becomes, by symmetrical displacement, the death of an academic opponent."[2] It is as if the doubling of mortal and god, European and native, disputed in the original colonial encounter retains the power to jam interpretation. Rather than intervene in this contest over the twice-dismembered body of

---

[1] Originating with Gananath Obeyesekere's essay "'British Cannibals': Contemplation of an Event in the Death and Resurrection of James Cook, Explorer," *Critical Inquiry* 18 (1992): 630–54, which stands as an assault on the fourth chapter of Marshall Sahlins, *Islands of History* (Chicago: University of Chicago Press, 1985), "Captain James Cook; or, The Dying God," this debate has been monumentalized in Obeyesekere's monograph, *The Apotheosis of Captain Cook: European Mythmaking in the Pacific* (Princeton: Princeton University Press, 1992), and Sahlins's book-length response, *How "Natives" Think: About Captain Cook, for Example* (Chicago: University of Chicago Press, 1995).

[2] Rod Edmond, *Representing the South Pacific: Colonial Discourse from Cook to Gauguin* (Cambridge: Cambridge University Press, 1997), 62.

Cook, I want to shift attention to what it obscures. Howsoever they disagree about the meaning of Cook, Obeyesekere's and Sahlins's accounts hold in common another symbolic body: the carnal figure of the ever-willing Hawaiian woman.

To make this argument I need to turn attention away from the fourth chapter of Sahlins's *Islands of History*, which deals with the death of Cook, back to its opening pages, which recall a day less commemorated in the annals of imperialism. On 7 December 1778, as his ships beat against the wind off the north coast of Hawai'i Island, Cook decided to lift the prohibition on intercourse that he had imposed almost a year before when anchor was first thrown at Kaua'i. As Sahlins dryly notes, from that moment the members of Cook's company were officially permitted to engage in what they had been doing all along whenever the opportunity afforded itself, having sex with local women.[3] Sahlins proceeds to analyze the structural profile of these sexual encounters in order to demonstrate that these two bodies—European male and native female—are symbolically counterweighted, the reification of the one heightening the desirousness of the other. According to Sahlins, the auspiciously timed appearance of Cook's ships, and their later sequence of departure and return, amplified the customary prestige of the stranger, and it was this coincidence combined with the cultural logic of *'imi haku* ("to search for a lord") which determined that common Hawaiian women would clamber aboard the British ships intent on seducing their company in order to capture for themselves the strangers' *mana*, or status.[4]

For Sahlins, the consequences of that capture were manifold insofar as the sexual invitation extended to European seamen by Hawaiian women irrevocably transformed the cultural order that engendered such desire in the first place. While reimagining the radically unknown as the desirably familiar, Sahlins asserts that Hawaiian culture itself "changed radically and decisively."[5] He makes no suggestion, however, that the European participants in these charged acts were likewise transformed through the encounter, and this is partly because of the way his own analysis might be said to refigure the new as

---

[3] Sahlins, *Islands of History*, 1–3.

[4] Sahlins, *Islands of History*, 24.

[5] This argument is first advanced by Sahlins in *Historical Metaphors and Mythical Realities: Structure in the Early History of the Sandwich Islands Kingdom* (Ann Arbor: University of Michigan Press, 1981), 33.

the old, bending the seductive logic of *'imi haku* toward the accustomed economics of solicitation. Inadvertently, *Islands of History* makes Cook's Hawaiian landfall resemble many another less prestigious disembarkation on which men, long confined to sea, secure the attention of women with a commercial expediency for which ports are already notorious. Thus the peculiar logic of Sahlins's sexual anthropology: the exchange of goods that develops across these sexual interactions will foundationally challenge the customary order of Hawaiian culture whereas it will leave intact the supposed sexual customs of seamen. The assumption of heterosexual exchange, an exchange that becomes more and more assimilable to the economics of prostitution the more it is enacted, naturalizes an impact theory of colonial contact whereby indigenous culture suffers an irrevocable change while imperial culture, like the stable accelerant that generates a chemical reaction, remains itself unaltered. To insist, as I am, that the forms of imperial masculinity, like the forms of native femininity, might be susceptible to transformation in these sexual moments is to promote a different understanding of Pacific encounter. Unlike the trope of contact, which serves to insulate a metropolitan culture from the distant societies over which it wields its power and contaminatory influence, this model maintains that the repercussions of encounter are felt by all its participants. Thus it might be anticipated that just as the locally specific sexual regimes of Hawaii are modified when they are extended to include the crew of the *Resolution* and *Discovery*, so too will the symbolic practices of shipboard life undergo significant modification.

It is worth tracing the logic of sexual contact within Sahlins's argument more carefully in order to see how his focus on a hypersexualized femininity exempts masculinity from change. The British, as their journals testify, initially perceived a vehemence in the Hawaiian sexual embrace that was without parallel. "There are no people in the world who indulge themselves more in their sensual appetites," wrote William Ellis, surgeon's mate on the *Discovery*. "In fact, they carry it to a most scandalous and shameful degree." However, Ellis also noted that this vehement desire was marked by a spontaneity and disinterestedness, so that "far from being . . . mercenary . . . some of their attachments seem purely the effect of affection."[6] In Sahlins's account

---

[6] William Ellis, *An Authentic Narrative of a Voyage Performed by Captain Cook*

the officers and crewmen on Cook's ships are, in this scene of arrival, unable to recognize the meaningfulness of their liaisons with the native Hawaiians. Indeed, it is only with the hindsight granted by the killing of Cook that anyone will see that the British themselves are transactable currency within a sexual exchange that also carries symbolic significance. Blithely ignorant of the extra freight they carry into this intercourse, the ordinary seamen rewarded what they saw as native surrender with gifts, only to have these gifts turn commodity and become themselves desirable. Sahlins writes: "Men brought their sisters, daughters, perhaps even their wives to the ships. Call it hospitality. Or call it spiritual hypergamy. The sailors showed their gratitude by giving the men iron adzes, beside what they gave the women. At the same time, the British trading with Hawaiian men for provisions found these demanding at least part payment in bracelets for their women."[7]

The gift in relation or response to sexual acts has results unanticipated on both sides. Once goods are accepted for sex, the gesture of courtesy doubles as payment, transforming the traditional pursuit of the stranger's status into a more pragmatic interaction in which an agreed value must be negotiated between all parties to the transaction, who now include the women, their affined kinsmen, and the sailors, who increasingly find themselves out of pocket in pursuit of what once was given for free.

For Sahlins, the significance of this hastening sexual trade is in the transformation it wreaks on a nonsexual but highly gendered order within Hawaiian culture. The advent of the British ships, and the daily exchanges that unfolded around their continued presence, facilitated an incipient relation between ordinary Hawaiian men and women whose interests came together in unprecedented ways. The Hawaiian tabu system—the cosmological prism through which traditional social distinctions between men and women, chiefs and commoners take shape—had traditionally defined the interests of men against those of women, but with the *Resolution* and *Discovery* in harbor, a rudimentary coalition formed which placed common men and women in opposition to the chiefly elite, who were themselves forging a priv-

------

and Captain Clerke, in His Majesty's Ships Resolution and Discovery, 2 vols. (London: G. Robinson, J. Sewell, and J. Debrett, 1782), 2:153.

[7] Sahlins, *Islands of History*, 7.

ileged alliance with the European officers and gentlemen. As the journals record, these concentrated developments resulted in scenes between commoners and chiefs marked by subordinate defiance and violent retribution. While relations among the Hawaiians became tense, with stones thrown and goods seized, the shipboard congress between Hawaiian commoners and British seamen relaxed into an expansive sociability that saw, most notoriously, the women's eating of prohibited foods in the contaminatory vicinity of men. The everyday improvisations engendered by contact with Europeans thus radically altered indigenous orders, in this case lending an increased urgency to traditional class rivalries and forging innovative identifications between genders.[8] "With transactions such as these," writes Sahlins, "the erotic commerce ceased to repeat tradition and began to make history."[9] The sex, as the structural anthropologists would say, was "hot" for the Hawaiians insofar as it involved them in historical change, although the implication remains in Sahlins's work that the sexual contact that unfolded in the Sandwich Islands across 1778 and 1779 was "cold" for its other participants. However vigorously the British seamen pursued sexual acts with native Hawaiians, it left their social and sexual regimes unchanged. It is this dull certainty that now requires critical reexamination in order to reveal that the gendered forms of British identity are no less mutable than those of the Hawaiians.

Refusal

It is helpful to restate the inquiry in this form. If the sexualized culture encountered by the British in the Sandwich Islands exceeded even the heated imaginings prompted by the earlier discovery of Tahiti, what might these unanticipated moments of erotic collision contribute toward possible transformations in the European sexual ordinance? Having come to second-guess sexual imperialism in the Pacific's New Cythera as the fantasy of heterosexual abandon, we should now turn our attention newly on not the sexual availability of the native woman but the sexual availability of the European man.

[8] Sahlins, *Islands of History*, 7–9. In *Historical Metaphors*, 46–47, Sahlins also draws attention to those violations of tabu that precede contact.

[9] Sahlins, *Islands of History*, 6.

If criticism assumes that ordinary seamen will be as inflamed by native women as they would be by the women in any other port, there is an equally held assumption that officers will hold themselves differently in such moments. The received critical portrait of Cook, for instance, is of a man almost asexual in demeanor, someone who stands removed or remote from the give-and-take of sexual exchange. In the penultimate paragraph of his biography of Cook, J. C. Beaglehole, having spent pages in subtle and precise speculation about his subject's genius, finally addresses Cook's sexual career, saying only this:

> He did not devote imagination, or emotion, or time to the other sex, apart from his [wife] Elizabeth, and from proposing, it is said, on Saturday nights at sea, the toast of all beautiful women. Any reputation he earned in the matter in the Pacific was, however, not so much for an habitual iron disdain as for obvious age and impotence. The passionately professional man was an idea rather beyond Polynesian conception.[10]

In what must have passed as an urbane piece of writing just a generation ago, Beaglehole here manages to deflect the accusation of inadequacy away from the European toward the Polynesians, who have no understanding that the achievements of masculinity may take a measure other than the physical. But Beaglehole's apparent sophistication, secured through the invocation of Polynesian naiveté, is equally blinkered. His analysis of Cook's sexual refusal as professional sublimation would seem to remove the imperial commander from the sexual stage altogether, as if by being less than amorous he was not therefore implicated in the slippery lovefield that was the pre-missionary Pacific. Similarly, there is something a little too quirky about Sahlins's joking—at Cook's expense—that if the Hawaiian women wanted to sleep with him because they thought he was a god, he declined because he largely agreed.[11]

How are we to read Cook's apparent celibacy? Amid all that sweaty fornication, was he the less sexual for being physically circumspect? Or is his erotic reluctance, however diplomatic, better read as denial, as disavowal, and thus as signifying entanglement in those modern technologies of substitution that have come to describe what we mean

---

[10] J. C. Beaglehole, *The Life of Captain James Cook* (Stanford: Stanford University Press, 1974), 713.

[11] Sahlins, *Islands of History*, 3 n. 4.

by the sexual? Although we may now know ourselves as sexual subjects through impediments to satisfaction, which also intensify desire, we should hesitate before ascribing such a pathology to another time. However fascinating we find our sexualities and the tremulous or stubborn shapes they take, there is nothing inevitable about their historical emergence. In conceiving the history of sexuality, we gain little from making the past the back-projection of the present. Rather, earlier configurations of desire—and the modern formations they prefigure—must be thought discursively "not as a positive thing but as an instrumental effect, not as a physical or psychological reality but as a social and political device."[12] Cook's erotic profile and sexual cut must be determined, therefore, by his investiture in a culture different from our own, one that has still to batten down sexual possibility into the microforms of sexual identity. If we approach the journals of the third voyage with less diagnostic confidence, refocusing our inquiry on the male body as it is implicated in the erotics of encounter, then we keep open the possibility that they may record some inscription of masculinity that is not yet ours.

Inquiry

Throughout their time in the Sandwich Islands the British kept encountering young men attached to the train of the chiefs who acted as privileged intermediaries between themselves and the Hawaiian leaders they served. This "Sett of Servants . . . are called Ikany [*aikāne*] and are of superior Rank," wrote David Samwell, surgeon's mate on the *Resolution*, "and their business is to commit the Sin of Onan upon the old King."[13] The British were frequently dependent on these men in their interactions with the Hawaiian nobility, and they recognized that their sexual role in no way diminished their political function. The social performance of *aikāne* differed from that inscribed in Tahitian and other Polynesian sodomitical practices—practices with which

[12] David Halperin, "Forgetting Foucault: Acts, Identities, and the History of Sexuality," *Representations* 63 (1998): 110.

[13] David Samwell, *Some Account of a Voyage to South Seas in 1776–1777–1778*, in *The Voyage of the Resolution and Discovery, 1776–1780*, vol. 3 of *The Journals of Captain James Cook on His Voyages of Discovery*, ed. J. C. Beaglehole (London: Cambridge University Press for the Hakluyt Society, 1967), 1171.

the European voyagers were already familiar—in this emphasis on their political influence and in the fact that their sexual role did not involve gender inversion, transvestism, or effeminacy.[14] *Aikāne* are unquestionably men and, moreover, men to be reckoned with. For instance, most of the British journal keepers agree that it was the part played by Palea, *aikāne* to Kalani'opu'u, in the theft of the *Discovery's* cutter that precipitated the fatal events of 14 February 1779.[15]

Samwell is particularly fascinated by these intimate practices between men and by the failure of stigma to attach to them: "This, however strange it may appear, is fact, as we learnt from frequent Enquiries about this curious Custom, and it is an office that is esteemed honourable among them."[16] The discourse of custom invoked here cordons off Samwell into the position of reflective observer. His inquiries, persistently renewed, are motivated by interest but morally neutral, as if the actions observed make no claim on him. This proto-ethnographic observation is markedly different from his recording of the sexual availability of women at Kealakekua Bay, which provokes in him an urbane literary style that draws on conventional tropings of the Orient and places the British subject at the commanding center of these scenes of sexual provocation, as the presence of a sultan inflames a harem: "We live now in the greatest Luxury, and as to the Choice & number of fine women there is hardly one among us that may not vie with the grand Turk himself."[17] The ease with which Samwell holds the one sexual spectacle at arm's length while writing himself into the other is all the more remarkable when he goes on to record how his attempts to discover more about this male-male practice were met

---

[14] Nor, according to the anthropological work of Robert Morris, did the *aikāne* relation between chief and male favorite distribute its agents across an active-passive sexual divide. Robert J. Morris, "*Aikāne:* Accounts of Hawaiian Same-Sex Relationships in the Journals of Captain Cook's Third Voyage (1776–80)," *Journal of Homosexuality* 19 (1990): 21–54, and "Same-Sex Friendships in Hawaiian Lore: Constructing the Canon," in *Oceanic Homosexualities,* ed. Stephen O. Murray (New York: Garland, 1992), 71–102.

[15] The authority of the *aikāne* was noted by many observers on Cook's third voyage, but Beaglehole draws particular attention to comments by Lieutenant James Burney, Master Thomas Edgar, and Surgeon John Law concerning the aggressive disciplinary role Palea fulfilled among his own people. *Journals of Captain James Cook,* ed. Beaglehole, 3:491 n. 2 and 509 n. 1. On Palea's contributing to the death of Cook, see in particular the accounts given by Lieutenant James King and Captain Charles Clerke. *Journals of Captain James Cook,* ed. Beaglehole, 3:530–33.

[16] Samwell, *Account of a Voyage,* 3:1171.

[17] Samwell, *Account of a Voyage,* 3:1159.

with a reciprocal question from the Hawaiians, who "frequently asked us on seeing a handsome young fellow if he was not an Ikany to some."[18] Samwell's entry for 5 March 1779 goes further and reveals not only that the Hawaiians saw something similar to the *aikāne* relation among the officer elite of the British expedition but also that they made approaches of interest in these men. Kalanikoa, "being on board the Resolution to day and seeing a handsome young fellow whose appearance he liked much, offered six large Hogs to the Captain [now Clerke] if he would let him stand his Ikany for a little while, such is the strange depravity of these Indians."[19]

The British in Hawaii had no doubt what card Kalanikoa was playing; how, then, did they react to the sexual call? Nothing quite prepares us for Samwell's apparent indifference to this request. Neither his journal nor those of his companions ever betrays any fear that they are somehow implicated in this Hawaiian solicitation, however keenly the request is pursued or however close to home the inquiry falls. Lieutenant James King's journal blandly records that as the British prepared to depart in February 1779, "Terreeoboo [Kalani'opu'u] & Koa asked Captⁿ Cook very seriously to leave me behind; I had had proposals by our friends to elope, & they promised to hide me in the hills till the Ships were gone, & to make me a great man."[20] It is known that Koa was *aikāne* to Kalani'opu'u; it is also known that both "Cook and King exchanged names with Kalani'opu'u and [another of] his *aikāne* Palea, respectively, in the Tahitian manner," though what that might have meant to the Hawaiians—who do not have such name exchange—confounds analysis.[21] There is only King's subsequent redaction of these lines when the record of the voyage was prepared for publication, which adds that the chiefs took him for Cook's son, and concludes that "the Captain, to avoid giving a positive refusal, to an offer so kindly intended, told them, that he could not part with me, at that time, but that he should return to the island next year, and would then endeavour to settle the matter to their satisfaction."[22] Is King's Cook being diplomatic or debonair? In both versions the British seem utterly unembarrassed by the request, and throughout their time among the Hawaiians—both before and after Cook's death—the

<hr>

18 Samwell, *Account of a Voyage,* 3:1171–72.
19 Samwell, *Account of a Voyage,* 3:1226.
20 *Journals of Captain James Cook,* ed. Beaglehole, 3:518–19.
21 Morris, "*Aikāne,*" 39. See also Sahlins, *Islands of History,* 2 n. 2.
22 *Journals of Captain James Cook,* ed. Beaglehole, 3:519 n. 1.

British, perhaps despite themselves, perhaps not, kept signaling this particular sexual availability.

If these journals record the visibility of the European male body to Hawaiian male desire, it does not seem to be a visibility that made these Englishmen squirm. What to make, then, of these moments the journals record when something appears to be going on between the Hawaiians and the British that looks strangely like male–male sexual recruitment but does not so much as raise a blush to the eighteenth-century cheek? The suggestion given by the Hawaiians, who see a similarity where Samwell, for instance, can see only a customary difference, raises the possibility that the ostensibly nonsexual professional relations among the officers of Cook's expedition might indeed have a sexual underside. It is my argument that although cross-cultural solicitations between Hawaiian and European men escape sexual definition, registering neither pleasure nor menace, the same cannot be said of relations between British men.

When Beaglehole, as editor and biographer, reflects on the character of the men who accompany Cook, it is "the intellectual of the voyage," Lieutenant King, who is most tellingly described:

> In 1776 in his mid-twenties . . . he had both naval and political connections. . . . He had read all the books; he could think for himself. . . . His technical duties kept him from wandering as widely as some of his colleagues. This was made up for not merely by his quickness and literacy in recording what he did see, but also by the sympathetic attractiveness of his character, which more than once made him an invaluable delegate for Cook—so that in Hawaii he was even to be taken for Cook's son. There must have been an almost youthful charm about King, a certain refinement of mind and of body, a humanity, a kindness, a generosity and sensitivity of spirit without touch of the effeminate, unusual among seamen—or amongst men: the combination of qualities that led the ardent young midshipman Trevenen to write of him (we must allow for the idiom of the age), "In short, as one of the best, he is one of the politest, genteelest, & best-bred men in the world."[23]

The "idiom" deployed, no less Beaglehole's than that of the "ardent" James Trevenen, testifies to the affective force of relations between British men. Although the naval officers of Cook's expedition reject or

[23] Beaglehole, *Life of Cook*, 496–97.

deflect the suggestion that relations among themselves are comparable to those between chiefs and *aikāne*, the terms of similarity are several: both are intensely hierarchical, politically and socially charged, and defended from the inroads of femininity. It is not that alliances between British naval men, or the structures of emulation they inhabit, bear no relation to power and social advancement but that the part that affect plays in such a homosocial system is less than straightforward. Shipboard relations microcosmically portray an institutional regime wherein masculine preferment or favor, undisguised by the rivalry for women, is sometimes the slick conduit for professional advancement, sometimes its scandalous ruin. These countersided effects will be distributed across two members of Cook's company, in their careers and subsequent reputations: Lieutenant King and Master William Bligh. The one, in Beaglehole's scholarship, will become the exemplar of masculine empathy and control; the other, in more popular discourses, that exemplar's inverse. Both men are better understood together as twin hostages to a discursively volatile disciplinary system that switches between the sentimental valorization of male–male relations and their stigmaticization as pathological.

Sentiment and Suspicion

When scholars of the third voyage speak of the death of the captain, they mean Cook, who, by that name or another, Lono, died on the beach a baffled man.[24] Interpretation, it sometimes seems, must fell him over and over again, as though it could not bear he die confused. In the calendar of that voyage there is another captain's death, enacted not this time on shifting sand but at sea in the cloying confines of a cabin. If Cook played two roles at once and stumbled in Kealakekua Bay over superimposed lines, his understudy, Lieutenant Charles Clerke, did not mismanage his own final scene. Promoted commander of the voyage on the death of Cook, the tubercular Clerke died only five months later and fifty degrees farther north. Readying himself for death, the weakened man dictated a final letter to his patron, Joseph Banks. Unsurprisingly, the role of amanuensis was taken by King.

---

[24] For a simple introduction to the doubling of Cook and Lono, the Hawaiian fertility god, see Beaglehole, *Life of Cook*, 657–60.

Such a formal tableau—the dying Clerke recommending the transcribing King to a second, absent, friend—is not lost on Beaglehole. The letter so written is, confides Beaglehole, "the document that carries most pathos in all the records of these voyages."[25] Clerke, he tells us, gathers his last strength to mark with his signature the subscription "your devoted affectionate and departing Servant."[26] Beaglehole is sympathetically echoing King, who writes of Clerke's slow demise, "Never was a decay, so melancholy & gradual."[27] In both the historical moment and the biographical revisiting, a lachrymose male gaze falls across the bedridden body of the fading Clerke so that the scene starts to swim and the chilly search for the Northwest Passage takes on the lambent warmth of a sentimental journey.

Whether or not we grow into its scholars, we are all the schoolchildren of imperialism. As all will recognize, the *Resolution*'s muster includes more than one household name: on his third voyage, as in a jumbled lesson, Captain Cook sailed with Captain Bligh. Master Bligh then, although Beaglehole, at least, can tell the kind of captain he would become: "Of undoubted capacity and goodwill and a first-rate sailor, but hasty and violent both in speech and manner, vain, and too self-confident and self-righteous to deal successfully with opposition or with difficult human problems."[28] Consider Beaglehole's account of relations between Bligh and King:

Not even this admired person, however, could be universally admired. It is not clear whether the master, William Bligh, detested him or merely held him in contempt: to Bligh, anyhow, he seems to have been, at best, a hypocritical and pretentious poseur. Why Bligh should feel so strongly in this way one can but guess: perhaps King was simply too small-bodied, too well-bred, too genteel, for a young man who even then, it seems, affected brusqueness, who may have considered himself a tar; who never, so far as we know, earned hostility by being polite; whose vanity may have been affronted by the very modesty of the other. We find no counter feeling in any words of King.

There may have been "something about" Bligh.[29]

---

25 Beaglehole, *Life of Cook*, 682.
26 *Journals of Captain James Cook*, ed. Beaglehole, 3:1542–44.
27 *Journals of Captain James Cook*, ed. Beaglehole, 3:700 n. 1.
28 *Journals of Captain James Cook*, ed. Beaglehole, 3:1465.
29 *Journals of Captain James Cook*, ed. Beaglehole, 3:lxxvii–viii.

If his King smolders with more than a seaman's felicity, Beaglehole's Bligh burns with "something" beyond professional resentment. Just what that might be is not anyone's guess: it is *everyone's* guess. What Beaglehole doesn't quite insinuate can't be insinuated enough. If there is a creepy shadow cast across these lines, it is not homosexuality but the suspicion of it. It is not that Beaglehole can't say what he thinks—that Bligh might have been queer—but that through such obscure accusation, homosexuality emerges. Suspicion makes a place for the homosexual; it is the vapor through which he appears.

In this way does Beaglehole's attractive Lieutenant King prefigure not just Fletcher Christian—another young man of gentility destined to be held in Bligh's attentive contempt—but those other handsome men handed down to us by the multiple retellings of Pacific history: Clark Gable, Marlon Brando, and Mel Gibson. The fascination with Bligh's special "something" and the men on which it was sharpened has not been confined to naval history or to the boys' stories that comprise imperialism's literary genres but has left its mark on the history of film as well. In the original production of *Mutiny on the Bounty* the Hollywood sex idol Gable plays a loose-limbed Christian to Charles Laughton's Dickensian Bligh. Nearly thirty years later, in the Technicolor remake, the ideological task is rather different: Trevor Howard's abusive Bligh is called on to make an Englishman of Brando's foppish Christian. Finally, in 1984 the ratchet focus of Roger Donaldson's *The Bounty* admits an interest in that unvoiced suspicion that has animated its antecedents and, to a certain extent, this chapter. In this latest—but surely not the last—celluloid retelling of the *Bounty* story, Bligh is thoroughly pathologized as a wet-lipped Anthony Hopkins putting the make on the blue-eyed, pony-tailed Gibson.

Policing

Though marginal to events at Kealakekua Bay, the figure of Cook's third mate has continued to magnetize attention across two hundred years. As the leader of a later Pacific cruise, Bligh's infamy lies in the way he keeps running foul of the intracultural prohibition against desirous relations between men and the directive toward homosocial intensity with which it goes hand in hand. That is the "something" about, if not Bligh, then at least *Bounty* interpretation that is so remarkable: if it can't quite say that what ties Bligh and Christian is thwarted homoeroticism, it can't quite say that it isn't. Or it has to say it over and over again. *Bounty* historians have successfully refuted the accusation that Bligh was a vicious tyrant, being less fond of the lash than the unimpeachable Cook, but they are unable to shuck off the suspicion that if ever Bligh whipped his men, it was because he loved them not too little but too much. *Bounty* criticism, even at its best, can still snag on the reversibility of William Bligh. If in Greg Dening's otherwise exhaustive analysis of Bligh's social indiscretion the reference to homosexuality is never more than an allusion, all subsequent readings of the *Bounty* depart from him precisely to the degree that they more thoroughly engage questions of sexuality.[30] Edmond, for instance, traces the origins of the mutiny to Bligh's inability to read the desires of his men, so obscure do his own remain to him. While the members of his company give themselves over to the manifold sexual pleasures offered by Tahiti, Bligh struggles with a far more truculent love object: the dead Cook. Bligh's "obsessive and neurotic" behaviors, in Edmond's account, manifest his "psychological dependence" not on any of the officers or sailors around him but on Cook as an internalized "father figure" whose "performative" afterlife in the islands of the Pacific keeps derailing Bligh's mortal authority. Bligh's oedipal drama—his attempt to emulate the captain in order to take his place—is thwarted in part by the inhabitants of the Pacific, who don't much care whether Cook is alive or dead but insist that all later visiting ships, and their various commanders hapless or deft, defer to him.[31] Under critical scrutiny, male rivalry and attraction turn out to have the identical function: both bond men. What this serves to imply is not that Bligh was homosexual but that identifications between men can always be read either way. Although this might seem a peculiar way of reading male relations, it is the one that insidiously comes to us as second nature. We could do worse than call this a homophobic hermeneutic; it is a regime that describes all of us, though differently. As a form of discursive policing, it regulates all relations between men.

Consider the Articles of War. As everyone knows, though I think we must have learned this outside the classroom, sodomy is a hanging of-

---

[30] See Greg Dening, *Mr. Bligh's Bad Language: Passion, Power, and Theatre on the Bounty* (Cambridge: Cambridge University Press, 1992), 8–9.

[31] Edmond, *Representing the South Pacific*, 65–66.

fense. The Articles said as much, and Cook had cause to read them to his assembled men on his return to the Sandwich Islands in November 1778: "If any Person in the Fleet shall commit the unnatural and detestable Sin of Buggery or Sodomy with Man or Beast, he shall be punished with Death by the Sentence of a Court-martial."[32] Yet as far as the records reflect, no seaman or officer who sailed with Cook was ever punished for sodomy. What of this seeming contradiction? Whenever it analyzes sodomy trials, many of which were naval courts-martial, gay historiography that thinks in terms of the oppression of a homosexual subclass, however emergent, has difficulty accounting for the relative infrequency of prosecution and conviction just it has some difficulty accounting for the elasticity of the category of sodomy throughout the long eighteenth century.[33] The Articles of War, for example, are in this instance invoked in order maintain a tight shipboard regime against the ancillary activities that threaten it, namely the sexual congress between the company and local women that erupted whenever the British ships were at anchor. Yet at the same time, every last man on Cook's ships was subject to an incipient disciplinary system that was redefining sodomy as the discursive limit for masculine proprieties, a limit that extended beyond the vilification and stigmatization of mere bodily capacities for pleasure, say buggery, into a more diffuse and subtle understanding of proper configurations of masculine sexual identity. Furthermore, this discursive transformation of sodomy—from buggery toward homosexuality, let us say—was accelerated through exposure to Polynesian same-sex sexual practices. In this context we might also recall that the Articles of War, however prohibitive, rely on detection for enforcement, not subjection, and it is subjection—not detection—which Foucault has taught is the mechanism of control deployed by modern disciplinary systems, systems that have at their subtle heart the sexualization of subjectivity. The Articles stand as the exemplar of an older power regime that targets and spectacularly punishes recalcitrant bodies (and pleasures) via mar-

---

[32] Article XXIX of the Articles of War, revised 1749. *Articles of War: The Statutes Which Governed Our Fighting Navies, 1661, 1749, and 1886*, ed. N. A. M. Rodger (Homewell, Hampshire: Kenneth Mason, 1982).

[33] See, for instance, Arthur N. Gilbert, "The *Africaine* Courts Martial: A Study of Buggery and the Royal Navy," *Journal of Homosexuality* 1 (1974): 111–22, and "Buggery and the British Navy, 1700–1861," *Journal of Social History* 10 (1976): 72–98.

tial codes of flogging and execution.[34] But when male conduct is structured through suspicion, at any moment, any relation between men can be invaded by the accusation of excess. Lieutenant King, for instance, has been wrenched by interpretation from a sentimental alliance with Captain Clerke to an exposure before a sinister—less small-bodied, less well-bred—Bligh. It is now commonplace to argue that between the gothic and the sentimental, the eighteenth century saw the opening of a representational space from whence some hundred years later the modern homosexual would emerge, but what is yet to be acknowledged is the way these effects are manifestly indexed to Pacific colonial discourse.[35]

Lure

Though never charged with sodomy, Bligh's bottom has nonetheless had its day in court. In the naval court-martial proceedings executed after the *Bounty*'s mutiny, reference was made to the half-dressed disarray in which Bligh was dragged from his cabin in the early hours of 28 April 1789, his shirt lifted high behind him. In Dening's more sympathetic account of those events, Bligh, manhandled by his crew, appears "bare-arsed, his nightshirt caught in the ropes that bound his

[34] My argument is counter, therefore, to that advanced by Neil Hegarty, who takes the Articles of 1749 to clearly signify that "it was misdemeanours in the arena of sexuality that were most savagely punished and sexuality that was constructed as the most uncontrollable area of human experience, the most prone to deviance." Hegarty, "Unruly Subjects: Sexuality, Science, and Discipline in Eighteenth-Century Pacific Exploration," in *Science and Exploration in the Pacific: European Voyages to the Southern Oceans in the Eighteenth Century*, ed. Margarette Lincoln (Woodbridge, Suffolk: Boydell Press in association with the National Maritime Museum, 1998), 186. Hegarty's essay—which elsewhere makes many fine points about how the records of eighteenth-century voyages register inconsistencies within regimes of power presumed to be hegemonic—is an example of a Foucauldian-derived argument used to support an assumption about the history of sexuality that is fundamentally opposed to Foucault.

[35] That the eighteenth century begins, in both the declension and intensification of the homosocial, to structure the doubleness of male relations as always suspect and secretly corrupt is the influential argument of Eve Kosofsky Sedgwick, *Between Men: English Literature and Male Homosocial Desire* (New York: Columbia University Press, 1985). Specifically, my understanding of the discursive work achieved by sexual suspicion proceeds from her discussion of the "blackmailability" of homosocial relations (88–89).

1 William Minchin, *Sketch of Bligh's Arrest, or Governor Bligh under the Bed*
(c. 1808), watercolor. Reproduced with permission from Mitchell Library Collection, State Library of New South Wales, Sydney.

wrists behind."[36] Nineteen years later, as governor of New South Wales, Bligh was again pulled infamously from bed, and William Minchin's satirical cartoon, used to blacken Bligh's character in the Rum Rebellion of 1808, represents these matinal events to a public already disposed to think the worst of Bligh (figure 1). Showing the governor apprehended while hiding ignominiously under his cot, Minchin's illustration screens Bligh's backside from our eyes, safely displacing any perverse invitation it may have made onto the plumpness of the mattress above. Of course, Bligh's bottom is neither a critical presence nor a structuring absence in this illustration, or indeed in my argument. It stands, nevertheless, in metonymic relation to the male body, across which the distinctions between authority and disgrace are erratically ciphered. The handsome, tight-trousered guardsmen Minchin depicts arresting Bligh might very well be detained in their turn by the incoherence of that disciplinary order, for as my subsequent readings demonstrate, the long arm of that law reaches beyond

---

[36] Dening, *Mr. Bligh's Bad Language*, 37.

that still warm bed and those Sydney barracks and finds its man in other Pacific locations.

Naval authority—a disciplinary code that depends on the incitement of desires that might also corrupt it—thus becomes an allegory of a more far-reaching homosocial system whose volatility as well as strength is linked to desires that exist between men. The strange restrictions and dispensations governing men at sea can be felt across the Pacific archive. In a series of extended voyages, many of them marked by violent and sexually promiscuous landfalls, the disciplinary task of mediating and refining competitive (and desirous) relations among men proves particularly charged in Polynesian locations, where the desirability of the male body is foregrounded without shame. The Pacific voyage becomes the occasion for masculinist narratives animated by a homoerotic desire that must be defended against. Although the dynamics of European interest in the South Seas have always been assumed to be consistent with a heterosexuality as rampant as it is ubiquitous, these narratives suggest rather that relations of dominance and submission are negotiated anew in these fields under the erotic pressure of encounters between men.

3 Marquesan Encounter and Male Visibility

In the previous chapter I argued that the governing paradigm of Pacific discovery is heterosexualized, both in the original archive and in its critical revisitings. In the former this heterosexualization serves to naturalize encounter and lend its imperial agents ideological stability; in the latter it is more frequently taken as the very sign of the abusiveness of imperial masculinity that everywhere recruits a native femininity to the economics of solicitation. In both accounts the male European subject's desires are assumed to be transparent, aroused in the vicinity of Polynesian women and readily framed within existing tropes of male-female sexual exchange. These hetero-sexual templates are so conventionalized within the records of the Pacific that it seems they barely need interpretation. This heterosexual assumption, however, makes commentators indifferent to the way the very reinforcement of these erotic coordinates—a reinforcement that occurs from one voyage text to the next—legitimates imperial pres-ence in the Pacific. This chapter, which considers the Pacific experi-ence after Cook, argues that this legitimation is most thoroughly challenged by those homoerotic valences that are equally, if less ob-viously, the legacy of his voyages.

In the wake of Cook, and with the dissemination of the published accounts of his several expeditions, later voyagers enter an eroticized Pacific already so well trammeled that their travel is marked less as discovery than homage to their predecessor. This structure of respectful imitation is crucially performed in relation to sexual encounters that postdate Cook. In the decades that saw the opening of the Pacific a tradition of sexual ethnography is founded that relies on the observation of native behaviors that have at their center female subjects. However, to focus exclusively on these moments, as much critical revision has, is to miss that other, less coherent tradition in which the European observer, transfixed by the Polynesian male, finds it much harder to negotiate his own relation to newly defined relationalities of sex and gender.

This chapter finds both traditions of sexual observation inscribed within the record of the first Russian expedition to the Pacific, undertaken two decades after the death of Cook. The Russian accounts of the Marquesan Islanders reinscribe the descriptive paradigms set within the earlier texts of Pacific contact, but in being that much later, they must also reference the new phenomenon of the Pacific beachcomber. It is the less predictable encounter with this doubled or hybridized figure, the European male whose mannerisms and deportment have become like that of the native, that resonates with an erotic potentiality that seemingly challenges rather than legitimates the assumptions of imperial power.

Arrival and Return

In August 1803 the first Russian ships to circumnavigate the globe, the *Nadeshda* and the *Neva*, left Kronshtadt for the South Seas on a diplomatic mission intended to negotiate trading privileges with Japan. The Emperor Alexander's expedition, as its leaders were only too aware, came late in the day to a Pacific already inscribed as an object of European knowledge and interest. However, this Old World dominion across the Pacific was being challenged by American presumption in the region, contributing to the sense of expansionist possibility under which the Russian ships sailed. In this respect the Russian expedition was both belated and opportune, the imperial ambitions fueling it less important than the capitalist itinerary it set. The accounts of the voyage published by its commander, Adam J. von Krusenstern, and its appointed naturalist, George H. von Langsdorff, suggest that the Russians entered a Pacific sufficiently mapped and inventoried by their eighteenth-century English and French precursors that it held few surprises. The metacritical trope of the voyage is not discovery but return, and the Russians—more or less self-consciously—found themselves reenacting foundational scenes first transacted by Cook's company in these and other islands and represented many times since. These conventionalized scenes, most particularly those that reenact heterosexual encounter all over again, have become the genre pieces of Pacific writing, as if the necessary authentication of the Pacific experience lay in the reflective exposure to heterosexual abandon.

Lying off Nukuhiva for ten days in May 1804, Krusenstern, as far as he was able, scripted his encounters with the native population—sexual and nonsexual—bearing in mind those local knowledges that Cook through Hawkesworth provided him.[1] Although their only prior landfall in the Pacific has been Easter Island, this knowledge garnered from reading has the effect of making the Russians strangely jaded observers of the Marquesans. Krusenstern's actions the day after first casting anchor were typically facile. In order to prevent his ship from being overrun with "visitors" while he is onshore, Krusenstern records that he "fired off some cannon, and hoisted a red flag, when the ship was declared tahbu, and all trade immediately ceased." As an aside he notes, "I conceive it unnecessary to explain the word tahbu, which is sufficiently known by Captain Cook's voyages," the sources as well for the significance of the color red.[2] The nuances of "tahbu," elucidated in his next chapter, are thus subordinated to questions of efficacy and command, whereby the knowledge of difference can strategically preempt and disarm its operation. At that moment, in these enabled hands, ethnography meets contingency and is redeployed as the knack of the place. In the time it takes to run up a red flag, the Russian demarcates not just a spatial trespass, a no-go area, but a whole field of execution in which anything goes, where power is not only prohibitive but insouciant, soliciting recognitions, installing complicities, tracking across cultural borders, to which it becomes increasingly indifferent.

Krusenstern's mild-mannered intervention in the local, his return-

---

[1] John Hawkesworth's redaction of the *Endeavour* journals had been published in London some thirty years earlier. Hawkesworth, *An Account of the Voyages and Discoveries in the Southern Hemisphere*, 3 vols. (London: W. Strahan and T. Cadell, 1773).

[2] Adam J. von Krusenstern, *Voyage round the World in the Years 1803 . . . 1806*, 2 vols., trans. Richard Belgrave Hopper (London: John Murray, 1813), 1:117.

ing "tahbu" to its home as a twice-translated thing, suggests that Pacific encounter is as frequently structured as a repetition as it is a discovery. This aspect of the Pacific landfall is, however, somewhat beyond European control, as is also brought home to Krusenstern on his first morning in harbor when, at dawn, the Russian ships are visited by the chief "Kettenowee" and his suite of relatives. Despite the early hour, Krusenstern diplomatically received on board "the whole royal family" and ushered them to his cabin, where their attention was caught by an oil portrait of his wife and, "no less an object of their astonishment," a looking glass. Krusenstern's account of this visit goes on to describe how the chief's amazement at the artifacts of European culture is readily subsumed in the monotonous display of a native narcissism: "A large mirror, in which they were able to view their whole persons, must have been something new to them; and the king was so particularly delighted with it, that, either from vanity or curiosity, upon every visit, he immediately went into my cabin to this glass, standing before it for whole hours to my great annoyance."[3] The implied complaint is that Marquesan "curiosity" never matured into enlightened inquiry: over and over it returned its subject to the cul-de-sac of personal "vanity." The technology behind the mirror was of little consequence to the chief, who repeatedly positioned himself before its shiny surface; his interest remained unmortgaged to the how and the why of it all, and his not seeing everything but nevertheless liking what he did see—himself and, perhaps, the stranger's "annoyance"—tends to place the foreign commander outside the specular circuit of flattery.

Whatever the Marquesan chief's repeated posturing suggests—to Krusenstern's myopic eye, a spellbound preening; to an alternate view, a more deliberate irking—what is clear is how the representation of that action, now as then, can be tailored to fit a European fancy. Krusenstern glimpsed in his guest's behavior an infantile self-regard that could then be elaborated as a native truth and implied point of comparison between cultures. By the end of the passage the commander is blithe and bored, affecting an exaggerated impatience with native foible; he has eased himself into the comfortable marginality of the interpreter, off to one side, disengaged but thoroughly in the know.

And yet Krusenstern's account also registers his suspicion at find-

---

[3] Krusenstern, *Voyage*, 1:117.

ing the dumb show of savage and mirror played out in the crowded confinement of his own quarters: "It was not improbable that some of them had already seen such a thing, yet they all looked behind the glass to discover the cause of this wonderful appearance." This was not, after all, first contact, and so Krusenstern was aware of at least the possibility that these islanders might be as well rehearsed as he in the staging of encounter. This native fascination with the furnishings and accessories of a European exoticism is questionable: might not some of these islanders be merely simulating their wonderment? Disconcerted if not outright skeptical, the commander seems in his representation of these events to guard against the danger of being taken in; all his observations are caged and made to bear the impress of that "yet." The Marquesans are said to display "every symptom of pleasure and surprise," as though the very transparency of their response is voucher to its inauthenticity, an inauthenticity of more or less sinister intent.[4] In the overcrowded space of the cabin the most casual of gestures is significant, announces itself as a sign, and demands to be read for what it might and might not mean. Hypertuned to the mechanics of dissimulation, Krusenstern has an eye peeled for the involuntary tic that would give the game away. He cannot stabilize the object of his scrutiny, as there is always the possibility that he is as transparent to the native as the native is opaque to him. There is no observant position that the commander can take up which would be outside these dynamics of mutual interpretability. Krusenstern may keep his masculine composure throughout, but this self-possession is no less a display than the masculine coquettishness the native chief is said to put on before the glass. Performativity and inauthenticity define both sides of this mirror scene and reveal that paradigms of cross-cultural encounter, unlike those of contact, open up both sets of actors to a thoroughgoing self-consciousness.

Sexual Know-How

With the already substantial published archive of Pacific voyages as his guide, Krusenstern has something of the canny traveler's obsession with efficiency and economy, with not being taken for a ride, and this

---

[4] Krusenstern, *Voyage,* 1:117.

determination extends to the way he will react to and record the sexual scenes his reading leads him to anticipate. In fulfillment of everything he has read, Krusenstern's ships from the moment they arrive are surrounded by swimmers who wave an unambiguous sexual semaphore in the direction of his men ("nor could they doubt that their wishes were understood, since neither their pantomime nor their attitudes could be mistaken").[5] Krusenstern, like many another captain before him, is concerned not to allow the sexual availability of native women to corrupt the discipline of his crew, and he immediately orders them to work on at their routines and issues "express orders, that no person of either sex, with the exception of the royal family, should be received on board without [his] permission." At sunset, however, once the male swimmers have all returned to shore, the commander rescinds this order and allows the dozens of women who still circle the ships to be taken on board for the night. In the published account Krusenstern frames this decision as his piteous response to the exhausted women, who have now been in the water more than five hours, but he continues, "I nevertheless set bounds to this favour, and, after the second day, no females were admitted into the ship." Not once but twice the commander changes his mind about the gender quarantine enfolding his ship. Extending a gentlemanly reach from the deck to the sea, Krusenstern gives his "consent" to the boarding of the amphibious females, only to indulge a morning-after regret. The next day the interdiction returns but this time reversed, so that women are now barred the ships but Marquesan men are seemingly exempted. During the rest of their stay, he writes, "every evening there were seldom less than fifty [females] swimming about the ship," so that each night "a few shots were fired over their heads" until they went away.[6]

It is unclear what sort of a sexual space this rather incoherent door policy makes for. Bouncing now this gender now that off the naval premises, lifting the color bar but installing a new vigilance around the commingling of the sexes, Krusenstern settles on a final order that reinscribes the social site of the ship as a boys-only club. Zoned exclusively for men, it is nonetheless defined, through heterosexual presumption, by the women it does not include. Krusenstern's about-turn over the presence of native women onboard suggests that the only sex-

[5] Krusenstern, *Voyage,* 1:115.
[6] Krusenstern, *Voyage,* 1:116.

ual proclivity that threatens naval discipline is that which involves cross-gender contact. Heterosexual impulse, presumed rampant in the Marquesan woman if not the Russian man, is therefore checked as a practice. It is, moreover, the only carnal activity that warrants policing. Other desires fall outside the commander's arrested purview. In this moment at least, naval authority turns a blind eye to cross-cultural relations between men that fall short of sexual definition, unlike relations between men and women, which consistently register both pleasure and menace and thus need reeling in. This structural imbalance resembles, of course, the situation of the British in Hawaii, whose sexual preoccupation with native women was matched by an apparent disinterest in Hawaiian men, most particularly those who professed an interest in them. But the Russian record also markedly departs from that earlier voyage, and as the Russians' stay in the Marquesas unfolds, what gets amplified is both the immunity under which the journal keepers pursue a sexual interest in women and the threat posed that immunity by the sexualized spectacle of men.

Krusenstern, for instance, is predictably self-assured when commenting on relations between Marquesan men and women as they betray the sexual exploitation of the one by the other. Thus he can explain that the nightly visitation made by the women to his ships is a sign not of their "debasement" or "ungovernable passion" but of "their duty to the unnatural and tyrannical orders of their husbands and fathers, who sent off their wives and daughters to procure small pieces of iron and other trifles." The gendered logics of prostitution comfortably enfold his own ships' practice but still allow Krusenstern to direct his contempt outward at native men, such as the one he observes "with a girl of ten or twelve years of age, probably his daughter, swimming round the ship and making an offer of her." As a commentator, however, he is both more and less engaged by other sexual events which have no precedent outside the Pacific but which have by 1804 come to be read as the authentic sign of a Pacific female sexuality.

Of the many incidents and manners he observed in the Marquesas, Krusenstern is most affected by the sight of a young girl engaged in sexual play:

> But what excited in me no less astonishment in a physical sense, than horror in a moral point of view, was a child not more than eight years of age, who shewed as little moderation in granting her favours as her sis-

ters of eighteen or twenty. I considered this unfortunate object for some time with a mixture of pity and disgust. In every respect a perfect child, laughing and playing with the feelings so natural to that state, she appeared not to have the least sense of her melancholy situation.[7]

Krusenstern records that he lingered over this scene "for some time," taking in at his leisure the significance of this display of precocious sexual competency. His representation of the Marquesan girl shuttles between the conventions of a hard and a soft primitivism; she is either slave to abuse or subject of unashamed rapture, and these alternatives fit the requirements of a hard and a soft pornography. Zooming in to focus on the "physical," catching the prepubescent body in frenzied embrace, then pulling back to accentuate the babbling delight of the "perfect child," the commander's vacillation leaves the native female the "unfortunate object" of his "pity and disgust." But perhaps we can look at this "melancholy situation" another way and ask how it is that this male observer can be so indifferent to the lure of nympholepsy, how it is he can be so sure that the excitation he felt, the "horror" and the "astonishment," were in keeping with "a moral point of view" and not indexical to a less blameless investment in the event. After all, the commander's scrutiny does not seem scopophilic, least of all to him. His commentary maintains the avuncular tone of the voice-over, and as a bedside manner, it is its own alibi; he cannot be guilty of an accessory arousal not because he was not at the scene of the outrage but because he was and—in all innocence—he told us so. A self-proclaimed voyeur, Krusenstern stands to one side of this carnality, and his concentration on the girl advertises the position of her sexual partner as a permanent structural vacancy. We cannot read, from Krusenstern's account, who the Marquesan girl coupled with, just that she did so and in abandon. Krusenstern's account deploys a first-person narration that sees and registers sexual difference but is unimplicated in that recognition. The gaze, in this heterosexualized instance, is the exemplar of a remote technology of power that subjugates its feminine object while insulating its male subject beyond the claims of desire.

[7] Krusenstern, *Voyage,* I:116.

Visibility

It is worth asking how this immunity from sexual desire is representationally achieved. The placidity of Krusenstern's account—the sexual quiescence it seems to ensure for him so that no matter how long and hard he looks at the transported young girl he himself risks no corporeal change or charge—is garnered through an intertextual affiliation. This eccentric moment is ghosted by other, similar moments in the South Sea archive and echoes a much-recorded event that occurred thirty-five years earlier during Cook's first landfall in the Pacific. In Tahiti on a Sunday in May 1769 Cook and his officers and crew celebrated their Christian Sabbath with a service inside the fort they had built to record the transit of Venus. As Hawkesworth retells it, on this day the Roman goddess, if not her planetary namesake, was fully observed:

> Such were our Matins; our Indians thought fit to perform Vespers of a very different kind. A young man, near six feet high, performed the rites of Venus with a little girl about eleven or twelve years of age, before several of our people, and a great number of the natives, without the least sense of its being indecent or improper, but, as it appeared, in perfect conformity to the custom of the place. Among the spectators were several women of superior rank, particularly Oberea, who may properly be said to have assisted at the ceremony; for they gave instructions to the girl how to perform her part, which, young as she was, she did not seem much to stand in need of.[8]

The scene in Krusenstern is too obvious a repetition to pass as an uncanny doubling; diminished as it is, the Russian version is none-the-less an explicit citation of an event textualized many times over under Cook's name. The episode recorded by Krusenstern appears simultaneously under the banners of authenticity and inauthenticity (it

---

[8] Hawkesworth, *Account of the Voyages*, 1:469. For Cook's original journal record of the events of Sunday 14 May 1769, see *The Journals of Captain James Cook on His Voyages of Discovery: The Voyage of the Endeavour, 1768–71*, ed. J. C. Beaglehole (London: Cambridge University Press for the Hakluyt Society, 1955), 1:93–94. Banks's journal entry for the same day mentions the divine service but not the profane. *The Endeavour Journal of Joseph Banks, 1768–1771*, 2 vols., ed. J. C. Beaglehole (Sydney: Trustees of the Public Library of New South Wales in association with Angus and Robertson, 1962), 1:277.

recalls an authoritative moment of Pacific encounter and at the same
stroke renders itself dubious, replaying that moment on another island
among a different people), but this is not so much a contradiction in
Pacific discourse as its necessary condition. Rod Edmond has recently
drawn attention to the supplementary function of textual citation in
Pacific writing, arguing that by the nineteenth century, "the elaborate
and repeated cross-referencing of the same few canonical texts in Pacific writing suggests" the "problem of authority and authenticity"
that beleaguers colonial discourse.[9] If the logic of precedence is dis-
turbed within and across many genres of Pacific representation, this
is especially evident when those genres are called on to represent divergent forms of sexuality.

For example, although Hawkesworth's version of this Tahitian sexual encounter is seemingly truer to Cook's original account, including a reference to the tall native man where Krusenstern maintains a
censoring ellipsis, it was precisely this kind of authentic detail for
which Hawkesworth's *Account* became notorious and unacceptable.
Cook was beyond suspicion in these things, but Hawkesworth was
not, and his *Account* was condemned by a metropolitan public that,
according to Jonathan Lamb, found in its particular mode of literary
representation a window to the brutality of an Orientalist desire they
had no wish to acknowledge as their own.[10] This irony is reinforced
by the narrational mode of the *Account*, which deftly collapses several of the journals compiled on Cook's inaugural Pacific voyage
and their variant accounts of events into a single narrative point of
view that is associated with the historical Cook. But the cover of
Hawkesworth's narrating persona is soon ripped aside as an outraged
public recognizes the tall native man not as imperialism's conventional scapegoat but as the author's literary prosthetic. Scapegoated in
his own turn, Hawkesworth is caught out somewhere between the
narrating figure of Cook, who stays out of view, and Oberea, whose
sideline interference becomes part of the sex scene itself.

If Hawkesworth's narration runs foul of the requirements of imperial discretion, the voyage account that appears under Krusenstern's
name keeps citationality working hard in the service of sexual inno-

---

[9] Rod Edmond, *Representing the South Pacific: Colonial Discourse from Cook to
Gauguin* (Cambridge: Cambridge University Press, 1997), 83.

[10] Jonathan Lamb, "Minute Particulars and the Representation of South Pacific
Discovery," *Eighteenth-Century Studies* 28, no. 3 (1995): 281–94.

cence. Otherwise almost a textual double for Hawkesworth's, Krusenstern's account edits out the native male to better serve both European taste and European fantasy. The moment of sexual representation is structured as a capsule repetition that secures an exquisite identification with an apotheosized Cook over the supine body of the native female. Removing the native male and attendant females, Krusenstern clears the stage, the better to establish the searing accuracy of his sightline, which concentrates its moral intention on the nubile child. Krusenstern shares Cook's imperial and heterosexual prerogative, to look on native females, howsoever young or mature, without avowing desire. Seemingly untouched by ecstasy or anxiety, the commander has defused the moment so that it makes no sexual claim on him. He is propped in an imperial posture: cool, disaffected, anything but amorous. In imitating Cook so closely, and refusing to be led astray by the textual extravagance of Hawkesworth, Krusenstern aligns himself less with the historical figure of Cook than with the structural position associated with his name, the vantage or point from which the view is taken. Cook, we might say, is the proper name for proper perspective. Crucially for my argument, this sexual propriety can be sustained only when the scene is heterosexualized, when the subject who looks is male and the object of that look is female. The peculiar gendered dynamics of visibility and invisibility inscribed in these scenes work to vaporize the position of the male viewing subject.

If the two commanders, Cook and Krusenstern, elide with each other in these scenes, it is even more significant that they both disappear into the technology of vision itself. The relations of visibility and invisibility inscribed here work less to corral the viewer into the sentimental precinct of the first-person narrative (which, according to Lamb, was what Hawkesworth's *Account* had been caught out in) than to win Krusenstern the unimpeachable jurisdiction of omniscience. As I go on to argue, this invisibility of the imperial male is also necessary to maintaining the abstract illusion of heterosexual privilege and exclusivity. As soon as the male European becomes himself available to sexual visualization, then he simultaneously becomes imbricated in circuits of desire which are more promiscuous in their effects and which give the lie to imperial omnipotence and abstraction.

Perhaps this reading of Krusenstern recalls Sahlins's line on Cook— that if the Hawaiian women want to sleep with him because they think he is a god, he declines, for much the same reason—though I re-

state it here only to suggest that a masculinity made safe by its denials
(here the refusal of desire and of the visibility with which it is associated) might be less of a joke than a loaded gun. Indeed, the Russian accounts of their Marquesan stay also yield incidents in which male
bodies become the object of visual interest, and these work to expose
the precariousness of a male self-possession guaranteed by its going
unseen. If there is a complacency to be heard in the Russian account,
it comes from the way certain events—and especially certain sexual
events—sound through the archive and announce themselves as rep-
etitions, as just what was expected of the Pacific. But this voyage also
casts up something the Russians hadn't counted on: the unknown and
visually spectacular form of the beachcomber figures who maintained
a fugitive existence on the margins of Marquesan culture.[11] Without
precedent in the archives of earlier voyages these male figures must
be read as sexual texts in their own right.

Punctuation

"Strangers in their new societies and scandals to their old," as Greg
Dening describes them, these male beachcombers—white sailors
who, having abandoned ship, stayed to ply a living in the cultural overlap of the beach—were inducted in a mode of cultural impersonation
that frequently lay claim to their corporeal selves howsoever they held
themselves apart: their material bodies were time and again made
available for sexual as well as cultural translation.[12] Indeed, repeated
intrusions on bodily space become the signature experience of the
Marquesan stayover, with the willingness of the beachcomber to allow his body to register this experience set against the difficulty of the
missionary to do the same. Frequently cited is the case of the recently
ordained William Harris, who was put down at Tahuata in 1797 by the
ship *Duff*, only to abandon his calling after a single traumatic night
alone among the inhabitants. Harris slept alone, having declined the

---

[11] The ranks of Pacific beachcombers are well catalogued in H. E. Maude, *Of Islands and Men: Studies in Pacific History* (Melbourne: Oxford University Press,
1968), and Bill Pearson, *Rifled Sanctuaries: Some Views of the Pacific Islands in Western Literature to 1900* (Auckland: Auckland University Press, 1984).

[12] Greg Dening, *Islands and Beaches: Discourse on a Silent Land: Marquesas,
1774–1880* (Melbourne: Melbourne University Press, 1980), 129.

offer of Tepaihena, wife of the chief who hosted him, but his sleep was invaded by curious women who wrestled open his bedclothes the better to debate the state of his penis.[13] Harris's sexual refusal is no protection against a comparative gesture that looks both first and last for a visible sign of difference that manifests on the body. However, the highly cited nature of this incident should alert us to the way it leaves in place as many complacent understandings of sexual difference as it unsettles. The timidity of Harris before these sexually voracious women is fully recuperable to a well-established tradition of Pacific sexual encounter that foregrounds the highly charged adjacency of male and female bodies.[14]

In the Russian account of the Marquesas, however, the familiar coordinates of encounter are crossed by another sexual system that takes its sign not in the bodily difference that Harris would rather keep screened but in the highly visible mark of tattoo. According to Langsdorff, what is singular about the appearance of the male inhabitants of the Marquesas is their "ornamenting their naked bodies . . . in punctuation, or, as they call it, tattooing."[15] As the Russian expeditionists are well aware, since the publication of the Forsters' comparative descriptive accounts of the islanders encountered on Cook's second voyage to the Pacific, the Marquesans have been celebrated for two things: the beauty of their physical form and, less wholeheartedly, their excellence in the art of tattoo.[16] Langsdorff, however, is so hypnotized

[13] James Wilson, *A Missionary Voyage to the Southern Pacific Ocean . . . in the Ship Duff* (London: T. Chapman, 1799), 140.

[14] T. Walter Herbert has recently offered a different reading of Harris's dishevelment and his subsequent abandoning of the Marquesas. The inexperienced missionary is, according to Herbert, thoroughly undone by this assault on his sleeping person, both physically and epistemically. Despite his vocation, Harris "becomes vehemently convinced that the Marquesans are 'savage,' because this ascription helps him to restore himself to order." Herbert reflects, more generally, that what is at stake in such moments is less the meaning of things than "our confidence that things are interpretable," that they can have a meaning assigned to them. Herbert, *Marquesan Encounters: Melville and the Meaning of Civilization* (Cambridge: Harvard University Press, 1980), 134–35. This imperative—to maintain the interpretability of things—is amplified in the record of Pacific encounter in moments when the ascription of sexual meaning to Polynesian cultures also forces the reinterpretation of one's own.

[15] George H. von Langsdorff, *Voyages and Travels in Various Parts of the World, during the Years 1803 . . . 1807*, 2 vols. (London: Henry Colburn, 1813), 1:116.

[16] See George Forster, *A Voyage round the World*, 2 vols. (London: B. White, 1777), 2:8, 14–15, and 30; and John [Johann] Reinhold Forster, *Observations Made during a Voyage round the World* (London: G. Robinson, 1778), 586–87.

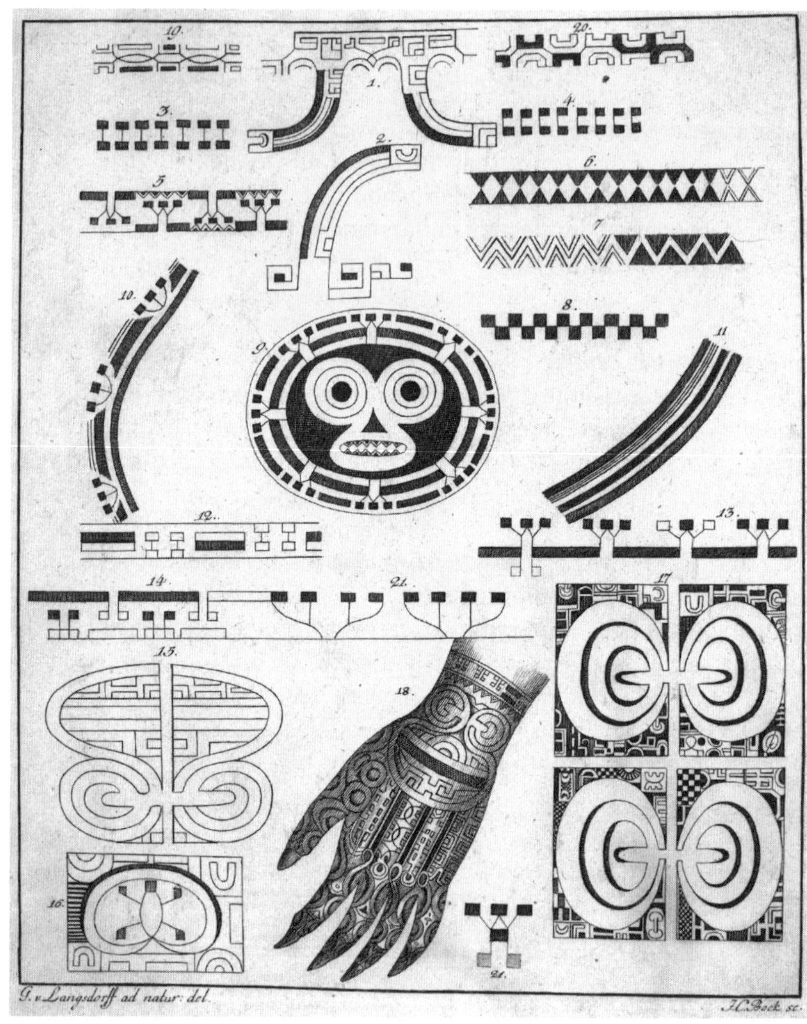

2 "Several of the principal figures used in tattooing, some in natural size," artist unknown, from Georg H. von Langsdorff, *Eine Reise um die Welt* (Frankfurt: Friedrich Wilmans, 1812), volume of plates. Reproduced with permission from Alexander Turnbull Library, National Library of New Zealand, Te Puna Mātauranga o Aotearoa, Wellington (PUBL-0184-09).

by the effect of this art that he records his surprise that the "acuteness of a Forster has passed over the subject with so much indifference."[17] The Marquesan male with his skin-deep tattoo becomes the subject of the naturalist's analysis, which jigsaws the overall pattern into constituent parts that are recorded as units of a discernible code (figure 2). "Every figure," Langsdorff speculates, "has its distinctive name, and most of them are appropriated to a particular part of the body" and associated with certain events or states, such as those "principally made when an enemy has been killed or eaten" and those that are "a sign of wishing to be beloved."[18] If these punctured marks can be read as insignia, badges of merit, or tokens of commemoration, then this catalog of figures attains the status of the appendixed vocabulary: it is the key to a foreign grammar. But Marquesan tattoo speaks with a forked tongue. Behind the alien babble, the language requiring translation, the Russian can make out another, more recognizable language: the familiar Esperanto of the body.

Even aside from its crazed surface ornamentation, the native male anatomy frequently draws from Langsdorff admiring expressions of recognition. "The men are almost all tall, robust, and well made [with] such general beauty and regularity of form," he writes, "many of them might very well have been placed by the side of the most celebrated chef-d'oeuvres of antiquity, and they would have lost nothing by the comparison."[19] Marquesan men thus occasion aesthetic respect as the primitive models for classical archetypes. Langsdorff records twenty-three measurements taken "with the utmost exactness" from one "perfectly proportioned" islander who had attracted attention through "his extraordinary height, the vast strength of his body, and the admirable proportion of his limbs and muscles." On the return to Europe, experts in the "natural history of man" calculate that the Marquesan's vital statistics correspond exactly with those of "the Apollo of Belvedere . . . that master-piece of the finest ages of Grecian art, in which is combined every possible integer in the composition of manly beauty."[20] The abstraction of an ideal "manly beauty" from the savage male suggests the neutrality of formalism, but Langsdorff also records that when these native men are first encountered, the almost

---

[17] Langsdorff, *Voyages and Travels*, 1:116.
[18] Langsdorff, *Voyages and Travels*, 1:xv.
[19] Langsdorff, *Voyages and Travels*, 1:108.
[20] Langsdorff, *Voyages and Travels*, 1:108–9.

involuntary European response is a far more intimate and idolatrous gesture of touch: "At our first arrival we were very desirous of stroking our hands over the heads of some of the handsomest men; on which they betrayed symptoms of great uneasiness and distress."[21] Looking, it seems, substitutes the inaugural desire to touch, which is as unwelcome in the museum of mankind Langsdorff thinks he has entered as it would be in many others, though harder to police.

It is this strangely totemic body, totemic to the European as his own model of masculine form, that presents the inscriptions of tattoo. In Langsdorff's account tattoo not only signposts the native body as exotic cultural site but falls on it as a flattering chiaroscuro, making its classical shape all the more discernible. Tattoo, according to the naturalist, visually enhances Marquesan flesh, accentuating the contours of the male form and further defining its perfectly developed musculature and torsion:

> The figures with which the body is tattooed are chosen with great care, and appropriate ornaments are selected for the different parts. . . . The most perfect symmetry is observed over the whole body . . . on the arms and thighs are stripes, sometimes broader, sometimes narrower, in such directions that these people might very well be presumed to have studied anatomy, and to be acquainted with the course and dimensions of the muscles.[22]

The visual effect initially "displays much taste and discrimination," although "in later years, one figure is made over another, till the whole becomes confused, and the body assumes a Negro-like appearance" (figure 3).[23] Langsdorff's aesthetic preference is, therefore, for the partially adorned young man, who wears his tattoo like a full-length cosmetic sheath (figure 4).

This idealization of the Marquesan male body is counterbalanced and ideologically stabilized by a collateral denigration of the Marquesan female body. "It is highly probable," Langsdorff admits, "that we saw a very few only of the really fine and handsome women, and that most of those who fell under our observation were the ladies of plea-

[21] Langsdorff, *Voyages and Travels*, 1:134–35.
[22] Langsdorff, *Voyages and Travels*, 1:122.
[23] Langsdorff, *Voyages and Travels*, 1:123 and xiv.

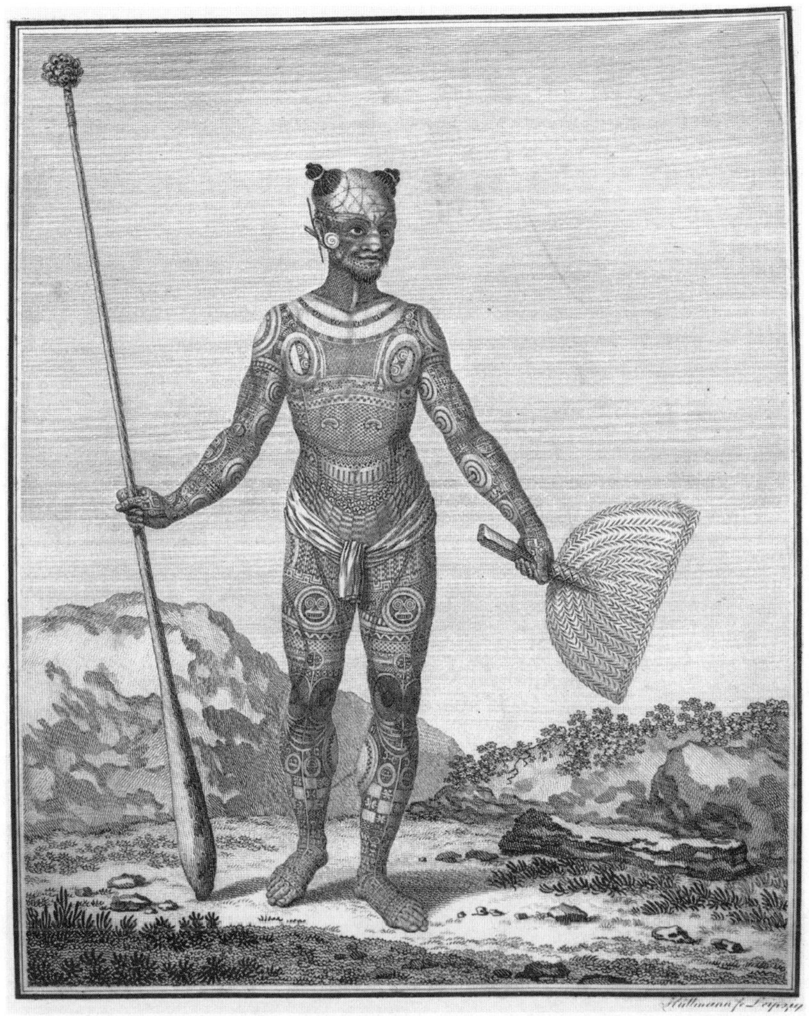

3 "An inhabitant of the Island of Nukahiwa," artist unknown, from Georg H. von Langsdorff, *Eine Reise um die Welt* (1812), volume of plates. Reproduced with permission from Alexander Turnbull Library, National Library of New Zealand, Te Puna Mātauranga o Aotearoa, Wellington (PUBL-0184-07).

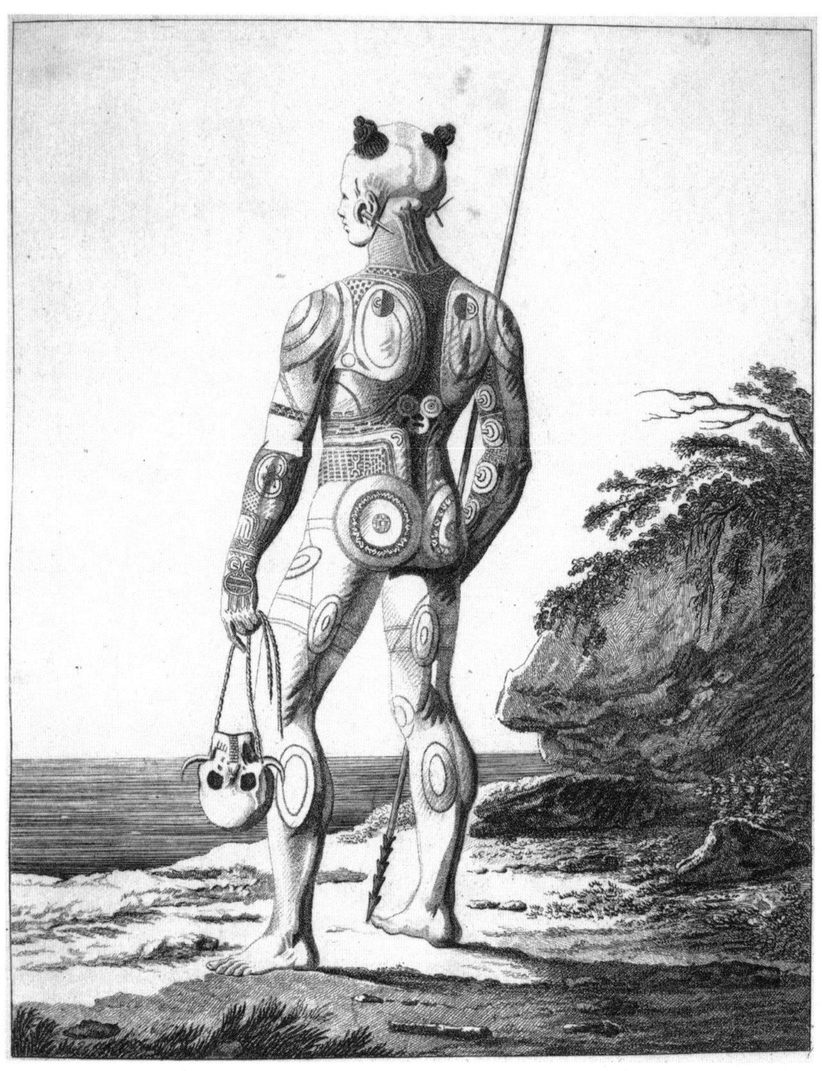

4 "Back view of younger inhabitant of Nukahiwa, not yet completely tattooed," artist unknown, from Georg H. von Langsdorff, *Eine Reise um die Welt* (1812), volume of plates. Reproduced with permission from Alexander Turnbull Library, National Library of New Zealand, Te Puna Mātauranga o Aotearoa, Wellington (PUBL-0184-08).

sure of the island."[24] These women of the "lower classes" are derided as "puny creatures, with bodies debilitated by premature licentiousness," making it all the more marvelous how such degenerate specimens, with their disproportionately large bellies and slow, trailing gaits, "could ever have brought forth such gigantic and finely formed men."[25] If Langsdorff fully renounces the attractions of this native female body, such repudiation seems tangled up with its being sexually available. The native male body, in contrast, is neither priced nor barred sexually and is the shameless object of Langsdorff's equally shameless address. For the European to exercise his taste in the matter of Marquesan male form is not to avow an erotic interest. The naturalist's gaze can loiter over this body without betraying intent; his interest in native men, like Krusenstern's interest in native girls, is untainted by the scandal of desire.

Jean Baptiste Cabri

Within the accounts of Krusenstern's expedition, however, appear more troubling figures, namely those European beachcombers who increasingly displaced the islanders as the object of Russian scrutiny and distrust. In the course of their stay in the Marquesas the visitors were introduced to two resident Europeans: an Englishman, Edward Robarts, and a young Frenchman, Jean Baptiste Cabri (figure 5). Both these beachcombers, vicious rivals in Marquesan tribal politics, saw the arrival of the *Nadeshda* and *Neva* at Nukuhiva as an event to be worked to advantage. Each maligned the other to the Russians, offering himself as the more reliable informant and interpreter. On appraising their distinct qualifications, Langsdorff favored Cabri as his

[24] Langsdorff, *Voyages and Travels*, 1:112. Krusenstern, in contrast, has no hesitation in passing judgment without observation: "Although of all the inhabitants of this vast ocean, I have only seen those of the Sandwich and Washington [Marquesan] islands, still I think I may say, with some degree of certainty, that the latter are not exceeded by any of them in personal beauty; and from the description in Cook's different voyages of the other islands of this part of the globe, their inhabitants will be found to bear no comparison with those of the latter group." Krusenstern, *Voyage*, 1:151. Once again Krusenstern strives not to be original but to imitate or repeat; the self-congratulatory Russian doggedly follows a known channel through the Pacific as if this trip were guided by the spirit of not James Cook but his namesake, Thomas.

[25] Langsdorff, *Voyages and Travels*, 1:112.

5 "Portrait of Jean Baptiste Cabri, a Frenchman, found on the Island of Nukahiwa, and there become half savage. He carries a slingshot," artist unknown, from Georg H. von Langsdorff, *Eine Reise um die Welt* (1812), volume of plates. Reproduced with permission from Alexander Turnbull Library, National Library of New Zealand, Te Puna Mātauranga o Aotearoa, Wellington (PUBL-0184-06).

guide because he "had lived much longer in the country, and had so much lost the manners and habits of civilised life, that little difference was to be discerned between him and the natives."

For the Russians the extent of Cabri's cross-culturation, his saturation in the Marquesan everyday, is marked by the loss of his first language ("He had almost forgotten his mother-tongue, and, at first, a repetition of *parlez français* was the only proof he gave of his nationality") and his affiliation by marriage to "a daughter of one of the inferior chiefs of the island," among whose family he lived "upon the most friendly and confidential footing." His induction into native custom is so thorough he is said to be inside not just native "habits and mode of living" but native "modes of thinking" as well.[26] But these twin credentials, while safeguarding his insider status, also fuel the scandal of the "French Boy."[27] In Cabri the Russians believe they have found an initiate in the ritual of anthropophagy. Desperate for witness, for a truth untouched by hearsay, they wish to wring from Cabri a participant's account of Marquesan cannibalism in order to settle the question of what befalls the victims of human sacrifice. Despite Cabri's testament "that he had never eaten the enemies whom he had taken, only *exchanged them for swine*," Langsdorff confidently claims

> that a man, who had in other respects incorporated himself so entirely with the natives, who might be said to be both morally and physically transformed into a savage, who himself confessed that he went out hunting on purpose to catch men, and exchange them for swine, and thought this an excellent pastime,—I cannot help, I say, being much disposed to think that such a man was very capable, when he had caught his prey, of eating it in company with his new brethren.[28]

The Russian naturalist requires Cabri to give evidence of the cannibalism of the Marquesans, as if the word of the Frenchman could establish once and for all the radical alterity of the natives.[29]

---

[26] Langsdorff, *Voyages and Travels*, 1:98.

[27] This is the phrase by which Robarts refers to Cabri. See *The Marquesan Journal of Edward Robarts, 1797–1824*, ed. Greg Dening, Pacific History Series, no. 6 (Canberra: Australian National University Press, 1974), 107.

[28] Langsdorff, *Voyages and Travels*, 1:148. On the word of Robarts, Krusenstern doubts this appraisal of Cabri. Krusenstern, *Voyage*, 1:168.

[29] The practice of anthropophagy has long served to set the epistemic limit that

Not only does Cabri refuse to provide this witness, but his peculiar appearance alone is suggestive of something more like a continuity between alien and familiar practices. "His whole figure," writes Langsdorff, "not excepting his face, was tattooed."[30] The descriptive representation of Cabri's tattoo reveals not a hard and fast distinction between savage and civil but their mutual interpenetration. In Cabri, the indelibly stained white man, Europe confronts not the unassailable difference of the native but the specter of its own discursive instability. This crossover body is imprinted with the trace of its own multiple legibilities. Langsdorff, for instance, describes Cabri as being "slightly and irregularly tattooed all over his body" and, like Krusenstern, draws attention to the symbol of the eye that encircles his natural one. Referring to it as his "black, or rather blue eye," the naturalist takes it to indicate his membership in an elite native society.[31] Cabri, as palimpsest, belies the rule of cultural identity and suggests that European bodies, as well as those of Marquesan men, are perversely resignified in encounter and subjected to a mimetic doubling that leaves then definitionally estranged from themselves, being both one thing and another. Alfred Gell, in his compelling cross-cultural study of tattooing in Polynesia, identifies one of the functions of Marquesan tattoo as an apotropaic "doubling" or "multiplication" of the person, designed to stave off both military and spiritual adversaries.[32] It is as if this unsettling effect is more keenly registered for the Russians when the markings of tattoo fall on the male bodies of their fellow Europeans.

A cloven man, Cabri became a more thoroughly expropriated body on his ultimate return to Europe. In the fluster of departure the Russians inadvertently carried him off the island:

Cabri was by accident obliged to leave the island. He was afterwards left by us at Kamschatka, whence he travelled over land to St. Petersburg. The extraordinary fate of this man, and the novel appearance of his tattooed body, attracted the attention of every one. Both at Moscow and at

<hr>

can demarcate the savage from the civil. See Peter Hulme, *Colonial Encounters: Europe and the Native Caribbean, 1492–1797* (Methuen: London, 1986).

[30] Langsdorff, *Voyages and Travels,* 1:98.

[31] Langsdorff, *Voyages and Travels,* 1:121–22. See Krusenstern, *Voyage,* 1:160.

[32] Alfred Gell, *Wrapping in Images: Tattooing in Polynesia* (Oxford: Clarendon Press, 1993), 197.

St. Petersburg he exhibited upon the stage the dances of the savages, and
was considered by all the great people of the country as a real curiosity.
Although he has by degrees become reconciled to European customs, he
still thinks with delight of the men whom he formerly killed and exchanged for swine, or perhaps eat. His dexterity in swimming, in which
he is scarcely excelled by the natives of Nukahiwa themselves, has pro-
cured him the appointment of teacher of swimming to the corps of ma-
rine cadets at Cronstadt, where he now lives. He has almost forgotten
the language of Nukahiwa, and made an incredibly rapid progress in the
recovery of his native tongue. The story of his marriage with a princess
of Nukahiwa, and the detail of his exploits on that island, are now so in-
termixed with the new ideas he has acquired in Europe, that any one
who heard him relate them would be disposed to think himself listen-
ing to a second Munchausen.[33]

Before being nudged into a line of imaginary voyagers, Cabri proves an
utterly co-optable figure. Spectacular freak or military adviser, he is
toy to the institutions of empire. His disparate knowledges, even as
they bolster metropolitan modernity, quickly fade into fictions. Unable to persuade anyone to sponsor his return to the Marquesas, Cabri
washed up in 1817 in the sideshows of the Bordeaux carnival, his cultural difference now mere transvestism. His career in the skin trade
had a postmortem supplement: he died in a hospital in Valenciennes;
and as "there had been some talk of preserving his unique skin . . . the
authorities had him buried between two other corpses, one above, one
below, to deter body-snatchers."[34] But Cabri is snatchable body still:
in most contemporary accounts he is elegized, his trauma and loss be-
spoken. In cruel exile from the Pacific, he trails a ragged poignancy
through the salons, fairs, and mortuaries of Europe.[35] Rubbed between

[33] Langsdorff, *Voyages and Travels*, 1:xiii–xiv.

[34] Jennifer Terrell, "Joseph Kabris and His Notes on the Marquesas," *Journal of Pacific History* 17 (1982): 105. Once again, Gell's analysis of the practice of Marquesan
tattoo provides another way for thinking about Cabri's embodiment of tattoo and its
redoubling of his personhood. Gell describes how in Marquesan mortuary rituals the
tattooed corpse undergoes desiccation rather than mummification. As the cadaver
mortifies, attendant women remove the skin of the deceased so that the stainless body
might "enjoy a desirable afterlife." Gell, *Wrapping in Images*, 213. Marquesan tattoo,
that is, was intended for posthumous removal: the flaying of the corpse marked the
appropriate and respectful end of the tattooed body.

[35] Those accounts include Terrell's, cited in the previous note, and Pearson's,
which keeps returning to a slightly melancholic account of Cabri's fate even as it

two cultures, his black and blue tattoo becomes tender bruise, sign of
a tropical sadness.

Visual Capture

The imperial gaze, so-called, has become indispensable to an understanding of the sexual dynamics of encounter; it lasciviously takes
as its object the female native, or in Said's originary account, it is said
to feminize the subaltern male as contemptuously effete. Above all, it
is a remote technology that leaves its male agent safely quarantined
beyond the reach of a returned look. The Russian fascination with tattoo, I have argued, bestows on the native male a hypervisibility that
is balanced by the abject spectacle made by his female counterpart.
But if in Langsdorff's account native men and women are subjected to
an enlightened scrutiny that seemingly brooks no response, other
moments in the Marquesan archive suggest that the possibility of a
sentient native gaze always haunts the scene of encounter, counter-
manding the ideological certainties and sexual privileges concentrated
in invisibility.

In Herman Melville's semifictional account of his brief residence
among the Marquesans, *Typee* (1848), the American sailor turns
beachcomber and experiences, as if for the first time, his own visibility. When Melville's narrator, Tommo, is held by the perhaps cannibal
Typee, he is not forcibly imprisoned, but his captivity repeatedly entangles dynamics of vision. Surrounded by luxurious half-naked
women and monumental tattooed men on whom he is free to look,
Tommo confides both the shiverings of delight and the shudderings of
fear raised by such a promiscuous spectacle.[36] Tommo's prolonged de-

______

maintains a critical distance from Cabri's own attempts "to present his plight in sentimental and heroic terms that might appeal to his European listeners." Pearson, *Rifled Sanctuaries*, 59. Cabri's post-Marquesan history has been reprised recently by
Vanessa Smith, who argues that the "performative relationship to [his] former identity" required of him on his return to Europe is continuous with the "alienated" performativity of the beachcomber identity itself. Vanessa Smith, *Literary Culture and
the Pacific: Nineteenth-Century Textual Encounters* (Cambridge: Cambridge University Press, 1998), 50–51.

[36] Tommo, in his time among the islanders, is debilitated by an engorged member—his leg—which swells and wastes, much to his consternation if not that of
countless vulgar readers who rely on the tumescence of Tommo's leg to hot-wire their

tention is marked by a manic shuttling between states of physical aggravation and lassitude, but what is equally notable is how his experience of anomie is indexed to being constantly exposed to native sight.

When the lame Tommo and his able-bodied companion, Toby, first enter the Typee valley, they are intimidated by the "inquiring looks" of the residents. When the two are taken into a large bamboo dwelling, "savage countenances" close in around them, "gleaming with wild curiosity and wonder." The perimeter walls of the interior are comprised of "open cane-work" through which those unable to enter stare in.[37] Encircled by faces rather than walls, Tommo and Toby, as objects of savage wonderment, have difficulty holding their composure. Their stoutness drains completely away when they find themselves displayed before "some eight or ten noble-looking chiefs" who, squatting close by, "regarded [them] with a fixed and stern attention."[38] Tommo continues:

> One of them in particular, who appeared to be the highest in rank, placed himself directly facing me; looking at me with a rigidity of aspect under which I absolutely quailed. He never once opened his lips, but maintained his severe expression of countenance, without turning his face aside for a single moment. Never before had I been subjected to so strange and steady a glance; it revealed nothing of the mind of the savage, but it appeared to be reading my own.[39]

The chief's penetrating stare proceeds from a body whose authority is reified into a gaze that cannot be returned, as if that look from which nothing can be hidden simultaneously makes its male bearer invisible.[40] Subjected to such a blank scrutiny, Tommo grows "absolutely

---

Freudian interpretation of the novel. In this context Paul Witherington remarks, "The leg cannot carry the burden of the symbolism any more than it can carry the narrator." Witherington, "The Art of Melville's *Typee*," *Arizona Quarterly* 26 (1970): 142.

[37] Herman Melville, *Typee: A Peep at Polynesian Life*, vol. 1 of *The Writings of Herman Melville*, ed. Harrison Hayford, Hershel Parker, and G. Thomas Tanselle (Evanston: Northwestern University Press and the Newberry Library, 1968), 70.

[38] Melville, *Typee*, 70–71.

[39] Melville, *Typee*, 71.

[40] D. A. Miller suggests that such masculine invisibility is historically the price exacted from men for heterosexual privilege. Miller, "Body *Bildung* and Textual Liberation," in *A New History of French Literature*, ed. Dennis Hollier (Cambridge: Harvard University Press, 1989), 681.

nervous."[41] The more silent and rigid the chief remains, the more Tommo compensates, offering first tobacco and then speech in an attempt to placate the malign undercurrent of this mute interview.

In the course of the narrative this "strange gaze," indicatively male, is eclipsed by the "pensive gaze" of Fayaway, the young native woman whose company Tommo keeps.[42] When Tommo is beheld by Fayaway, he sees in her eyes not inscrutable power but recognition, understanding, and "the liveliest sympathy," as if "she alone seemed to appreciate the effect which the peculiarity of the circumstances in which we were placed had produced upon the minds of my companion and myself." Her "large glistening eyes" gaze "intently" into his, but far from feeling threatened, he is persuaded by her manner that "she deeply compassionated" his situation.[43] Awash in self-pity, Tommo spends his time imagining that Fayaway's own is taken up giving fantastic shape and specificity to the cruel contours of his sentimental dislocation, that she is always thinking of things that otherwise claim little narrative space: the brothers and sisters he has left behind, the family who will be anxious for his safe return.

Where Tommo submits to the chief's arresting optic, matching the ocular self-effacement of the native with strategic abasement, with Fayaway such evacuation is not called for. Tommo can reassuringly project onto this native woman a reciprocating interiority, a vibrancy that can countersign his sense of his own sadness, his own loss. Tommo's desire for this mirroring regard becomes especially urgent after Toby leaves the valley. It is as if identity can be maintained only through technologies of interlocution, but where this can be achieved between men of the same stripe (two sailors, say), when a cultural difference intervenes it can be achieved only by arcing compulsorily between terminals gendered male and female.

Escape or Assimilation

If Melville's narrative can be said to record his hero's savage romance, however, that story has less to do with the obligations of het-

---

[41] Melville, *Typee*, 71.
[42] Melville, *Typee*, 78 and 134.
[43] Melville, *Typee*, 108.

erosexuality than the dubious and alternating attractions of passivity and aggression as they are experienced in relation to other men. Throughout *Typee,* Tommo is repeatedly pinioned by Marquesan men whose intentions remain obscure to him. In his final attempt to escape the valley Tommo is forced to cross the visual field of Mow-Mow, a ferocious Cyclops with a mutilated face who has stalked him throughout his stay. Mow-Mow's one-eyed obsession with Tommo baffles him with its vehemence, and it is only when his rescuer, Karakoee, "an Oahu Kannaka, who had often been aboard the 'Dolly' while she lay in Nukuheva," fails to buy his freedom with musket and powder that the would-be beachcomber recognizes the extent of his objectification: "When I remembered the extravagant value placed by these people upon the articles which were offered to them in exchange for me, and which were so indignantly rejected, I saw a new proof of the same fixed determination of purpose they had all along manifested with regard to me."[44] Alienated in some system of value of which he cannot take the measure, marked as eminently desirable but with no idea why, Tommo's response is telling: "in despair, and reckless of consequences, I exerted all my strength, and shaking myself free from the grasp of those who held me, I sprang upon my feet and rushed towards Karakoee."[45]

The shape Tommo's panic repeatedly takes is a forceful lurch that breaks the hold of one native man and delivers him to the safety promised by another. From the side of a retreating boat Tommo lashes out at Mow-Mow with a metal boat hook, striking his pursuer "just below the throat" and forcing him beneath the water only to watch him surface with a "ferocious expression" he is unable to forget. But even in violence Tommo's body is tremulous. Overtaken by emotion, swoon follows blow, as Tommo falls back into a final, accommodating, native embrace: "the next minute we were past them all, and in safety. The strong excitement which had thus far kept me up, now left me, and I fell back fainting into the arms of Karakoee."[46]

Yet the most volatile erotic encounter described in *Typee* occurs with none of these commanding male protagonists, nor with the insipid Fayaway, but involves Tommo and a third figure, Marnoo, a

44 Melville, *Typee,* 249–50.
45 Melville, *Typee,* 250.
46 Melville, *Typee,* 252.

tabooed outsider who enters the valley a privileged stranger. At first meeting, Tommo is entranced by this "beautifully formed" figure and steals a host of rear and sidewise views of his "unclad limbs" and "close curling ringlets." Marnoo's attractiveness resides in his "demeanour," which is as subtly marked by gender ambivalence as his face is spared the disfiguring scars of tattoo: "His cheek was of a feminine softness, and his face was free from the least blemish of tattooing, although the rest of his body was drawn all over with fanciful figures."[47] In the vicinity of this androgynous figure, Tommo is himself drawn toward gender-discordant behavior. When Marnoo first enters, Tommo "involuntarily" rises from his seat and offers the visitor a place. When his gentlemanly politeness is ignored, however, Tommo registers the insult not as a rejected male suitor but as if his own feminine charms have been overlooked: "Had the belle of the season, in the pride of her beauty and power, been cut in a place of public resort by some supercilious exquisite, she could not have felt greater indignation than I did at this unexpected slight."[48]

The narrative maintains this feminized conceit at some length. The magnetic charms of Marnoo, this "all-attractive personage," are such that Tommo discovers his own significantly weakened in their proximity, and he confesses that when he "observed the striking devotion of the natives to him, and their temporary withdrawal of all attention from myself, I felt not a little piqued." Rather than yield to Marnoo his position as object of all "curiosity and regard," Tommo is drawn into a rivalrous identification with him: "The singularity of his conduct, however, only roused my desire to discover who this remarkable personage might be, who now engrossed the attention of every one."[49] In the extended scene that follows, an exaggerated masculine jealousy takes on the conventional trappings of feminine vanity as Melville deploys sexual irony the better to pose an erotic invitation transacted between two men. Tommo's spellbound eyes slyly chase Marnoo's manifest charms through five pages of coyness before they are rewarded with the sweet delivery of a downcast approach:

[47] Melville, *Typee*, 135–36. Following Nigel Rigby, Edmond points out that Marnoo's name reinforces his association with transvestism by echoing the word *māhū*, which describes, in both the Marquesas and Tahiti, males who assume female roles. See Edmond, *Representing the South Pacific*, 91.

[48] Melville, *Typee*, 136–37.

[49] Melville, *Typee*, 137.

> At length, from certain indications, I suspected that he was making me
> the subject of his remarks, although he appeared cautiously to avoid ei-
> ther pronouncing my name, or looking in the direction where I lay. All
> at once he rose from the mats where he had been reclining, and, still con-
> versing, moved towards me, his eye purposely evading mine, and seated
> himself within less than a yard of me. I had hardly recovered from my
> surprise, when he suddenly turned round, and, with a most benignant
> countenance, extended his right hand gracefully towards me. Of course
> I accepted the courteous challenge, and, as soon as our palms met, he
> bent towards me, and murmured in musical accents,—"How you do?"[50]

This subtle come-hithering between Tommo and Marnoo marks the
desirable limit of Melville's Polynesian romance, overthrowing as it
does most of the behaviors considered natural to sailors when they are
not at sea but at the same time cloaking them in protective ironies as
thick as the counterpane that covers Ishmael and Queequeg lying together in bed at the Spouter's Inn.[51]

But whatever the manifest appeal of crossing over, Tommo also puts
up resistance to this Pacific trade. Melville's novel cannot allay the
fear, and seems not to want to, that what you see might be what you
get, or at least become. Throughout *Typee,* tattoo stands as merely the
final and most literal invasion of a white male subjectivity whose
boundaries have already proven alarmingly permeable, dangerously
susceptible to visual erasure and reinscription. Seduced by many aspects of Marquesan life but resilient to others, Tommo displays a thin-
skinned response at the thought of being tattooed. Fearing to tread
where other beachcombers rush in, Tommo demonstrates an appre-
hensiveness about being marked that might profitably be placed in
conjunction with Gell's analysis of the "paradoxical double skin" ex-
emplified in the whole-body tattoo worn by Marquesan men. "It remains," writes Gell, "important not to lose sight of the fact that the
skin and the tattoo are integrally one and indivisible." European observers were, he argues, wrong to think of tattoo as a second skin that
modestly cloaked the nude body. Rather, the enactment of Marquesan
male tattoo, *pahu tiki,* reveals "an inside which comes from the out-

---

[50] Melville, *Typee,* 139.
[51] Herman Melville, *Moby Dick,* vol. 6 of *The Writings of Herman Melville,* ed.
Harrison Hayford, Hershel Parker, and G. Thomas Tanselle (Evanston: Northwestern
University Press and the Newberry Library, 1988), 25.

side, which has been applied externally prior to being absorbed into the interior."[52] The double invagination of subjectivity effected by tattoo leaves no room for veiling, particular those literary veils that Melville routinely throws between his sophisticated narration and the naive Tommo who is its only mouthpiece. Were irony withdrawn, then all that stands between Tommo's male self and Marnoo, his effeminate other, is membrane thin. Gell suggests that there is no defense against the peculiar erotic pull of tattoo, as it inevitably draws a sexualized look from its observer. The threat of tattoo, he argues, is engaged visually rather than in its technology of application so that "to view tattoo is already to be in a position of seduction; it provokes, not an aesthetic response but a kind of bodily looking which is intrinsically sexualised."[53] This point is everywhere conceded by Melville's narration but remains something that Tommo is never allowed to confirm.

Divided against itself, Melville's Marquesan narrative entraps its straight narrator in cross-cultural dynamics of male-male identification and desire.[54] In *Typee* Pacific sexual encounter comprises not the romance between Tommo and Fayaway but those moments when Polynesian practices reflect back to a mortified European gaze a newly defined capacity for bodily perversion. Drawn to the South Seas by texts such as Melville's, later visitors to the Pacific will actively seek out precisely this experience, as if the undoing of European masculinity could be restaged on command. The next chapter first considers how, before this decadent impulse takes the Pacific as its logical destination, a Church Missionary Society cleric at work in the mission fields of early-nineteenth-century New Zealand can fall foul of the less than hard-line distinction between proper and improper relations among men.

---

[52] Gell, *Wrapping in Images*, 38–39.

[53] Gell, *Wrapping in Images*, 36. "Marked, patterned, or scarred skin," writes Gell, "draws in the gaze of the onlooker, exercises the power of fascination, and lowers certain defences. The eye isolates and follows the mazy pathways of the design and eventually, so to speak, enters the body of the other, because the peculiarity of tattooing is that it is inside the skin rather than on the surface" (ibid.).

[54] Edmond discusses how Melville's narrative constantly poses heterosexual and homosexual alternatives "with the heterosexual as represented by Fayaway dominant, but the homosexual in the form of Marnoo remaining palpably attractive." Edmond, *Representing the South Pacific*, 92. These alternatives are perhaps less stable and less distinct than Edmond suggests, not least because *Typee*, and Pacific texts more generally, is still engaged in producing them as complementary forms of what will come to be known as sexuality.

4 Sexual Difference and the Expulsion of William Yate

The subject of this chapter is not the historical figure, William Yate. Rather, it is the contradictory sexual meanings that have circulated in his name in the 170 years since he disembarked, a young, ambitious missionary, in New Zealand's Bay of Islands. Like another figure from Pacific history, William Bligh, Yate has been read differently from one moment to the next, appearing first as victim then as demon in a frequently retold story that engages themes of sexual betrayal within faltering codes of male discipline.[1] The changing accent in what we might term Yate's cultural legibility reveals not the final truth of his person but the different truth effects generated across his name from one moment to the next. Yate, in this understanding, is a placemarker, an imaginary figure of sexual alterity and similitude whose ambiguity continues to generate rifts in colonial narratives, to which he is always considered dispensable, the exception rather than the rule. The repeated shaming of Yate, and the way he is necessarily excluded from accounts of settlement, is crucial to understanding how such narratives work.

Yate was twenty-six years old when he took up his ministry with the Church Missionary society at Paihia in 1828. Six and a half years later, and without the leave of his superiors, he voyaged home. En

---

[1] See Greg Dening, *Mr. Bligh's Bad Language: Passion, Power, and Theatre on the Bounty* (Cambridge: Cambridge University Press, 1992).

route to England he took the journals he had kept since joining the mission community and composed from them *An Account of New Zealand and of the Formation and Progress of the Church Missionary Society's Mission in the Northern Island.* Published immediately, the *Account* secured for Yate both contemporary fame and a more permanent place in the documentary archives of New Zealand colonial history. In 1970 a facsimile edition of Yate's *Account* appeared that included among other supplements an introduction by the historian Judith Binney, whose published work has become the point of dissemination for the widest understanding of the significance of Yate's manuscript and its depiction of the relations between northern Maori and the Church Missionary Society in the late 1820s.[2]

Primarily concerned with the *Account*'s record of the activities of the Waimate mission and the Maori prophet movement that was gaining momentum on its periphery, Binney's introduction also provides biographical details about Yate that extend beyond his tenure at Waimate. In 1836, after two years in England touring and lecturing for the Church Missionary Society, Yate, intending to resume his activities with the Bay of Islands mission, once again sailed for New Zealand, this time in the company of his sister, Sarah. In June his ship, the *Prince Regent,* docked in Sydney, where Yate was asked to temporarily assume the position of chaplain at St. James' Church. "While [he was] serving in this capacity," Binney continues,

> rumours were circulated about him which prevented his return to missionary work and led to his dismissal from the C[hurch] M[issionary] S[ociety].
>
> . . . Yate was "warned" of gossip to the effect that he had had homosexual relations with the third officer of the *Prince Regent,* [Edwin] Denison, by two of his fellow passengers, the Reverend Richard Taylor and John Armitstead, a Sydney lawyer. Later, it was argued that "a mass of information" could be produced of similar relations in New Zealand, "of sufficient weight to crush a host."[3]

---

[2] Judith Binney, introduction to *An Account of New Zealand and of the Formation and Progress of the Church Missionary Society's Mission in the Northern Island,* by William Yate (2d ed., 1835; reprint, Wellington: A. H. and A. W. Reed, 1970). My indebtedness to the scholarship of Judith Binney is unbounded, as anyone who has trailed her through the tangle of documents pertaining to William Yate will know.

[3] Binney, introduction to *Account of New Zealand,* xvi.

In the weeks and months following Yate's return to Sydney, stories continued to surface which placed him in disturbing proximity to native youths as well as English officers so that his conduct in the mission schools of northern New Zealand came under as much anxious scrutiny as the relations said to have arisen aboard the *Prince Regent.*

On 13 August, Yate's clerical license was suspended by William Broughton, bishop of Sydney. Four months passed with an ill-coordinated investigation under way, but try as he might, Yate never succeeded in having his case heard before a proper tribunal. In mid-December he sailed for England, hoping to have the rumors more properly investigated, only to find that on the basis of information received from Australia, the Church Missionary Society had preemptively dissolved its connection with him. All Yate's attempts to have the case reopened and his character cleared were refused by the society, whose only response to these appeals was to permit its members to read the documents against Yate, all of which pertained to conduct observed on the *Prince Regent.* Although Samuel Marsden had collected material concerning Yate's behavior in New Zealand and Sydney, he neglected to send it on to London. These depositions remained in Australia, unseen by any except those involved in the original inquiry, and included four affidavits from Maori youth cross-examined by the Waimate missionaries which the crown prosecutor of New South Wales did not consider to comprise evidence of criminal wrongdoing.[4]

Binney's research reveals that over the next six years Yate "made three attempts by pamphlet to have his case investigated"; the final pamphlet, published in 1843, "contained a massive amount of evidence on his behalf, including a signed retraction of the original 'scandalous' reports taken from the first mate of the *Prince Regent* by [the lawyer] Armitstead, for the price of a *'bucket of ale.'*"[5] None of this lobbying impressed the Church Missionary Society or the bishop of London, who brought down a prohibition around the ex-missionary that prevented him from holding a living in the British Isles. Yate, according to Binney, maintained throughout his life "that the whole affair had been an 'unprincipled conspiracy' against him, to deprive him of the attractive position at St James, in favour of Taylor, and to take revenge for his rejection of both Taylor and Armitstead socially, when

---

[4] See Binney, introduction to *Account of New Zealand,* xvii–xviii.
[5] Binney, introduction to *Account of New Zealand,* xviii.

he reached the colony and his friends." With the forensic reconstruction complete, Binney weighs up the accusations, revelations, and outcomes that hedged around Yate. In this context she cites Richard
Taylor, one of the original shipboard informers, who concluded that
although to his mind Yate was "guilty of the grossest indecency of
character," he could not be accused of any "actual crime," before
drawing a somewhat different inference of her own: "The most probable verdict seems to be that although Yate was emotionally inclined
to homosexuality, he was innocent of the physical act."[6]

Evidence

When the facsimile edition of *An Account of New Zealand* appeared, Binney's introductory essay drew critical attention from Frank
Sargeson, who immediately challenged the reference to Yate's probable homosexuality on the grounds that "the use of 'homosexual' is
very questionable: the word was not invented until the late nineteenth
century" and called for the restitution of the "exact terms used by Taylor and Armitstead."[7] Sargeson is correct about the advent of the word
homosexual, but this shouldn't blind us to the fact that his review is
as charged by the contemporary resonance of the term in the early
1970s as it is by its historical antecedents. In a letter to *Landfall* Binney responds that she had avoided the historically accurate term
sodomy because of its "biblical authority" and implies that she favored *homosexual* as preserving the several moral ironies engaged by
Yate's case and the conduct of his chief "accuser," Taylor.[8] It should
not surprise us that the liberal impulse that fuels this particular ob-
fuscation (historical and moral) goes unthanked by Sargeson, who
lived out many of the contradictions it continues to support. Sargeson's homosexuality has long been the open secret of New Zealand letters, variously known, ignored, or accepted across several generations
of readership. The same might be said of his fiction, which deftly
mines the strained terms by which male–male erotics are contracted

---

[6] Binney, introduction to *Account of New Zealand*, xix.

[7] Frank Sargeson, review of *An Account of New Zealand and of the Formation and
Progress of the Church Missionary Society's Mission in the Northern Island*, by
William Yate, *Landfall* 25, no. 3 (1971): 302–3.

[8] Judith Binney, letter in *Landfall* 25, no. 4 (1971): 473–74.

within a culture that has no wish to own them but every wish to expose, exploit, or sublimate them.

Historically, the epistemological and social space through which the difficult relation between the avowal and denial of homosexuality has been written and lived has gone by the name of the closet. If Sargeson, as fully as his fictional characters, is entangled in these problematics of sexual knowledge and secrecy, his critics as well do not easily escape them.[9] In his intervention in the Yate debate Kendrick Smithyman, for example, directs his impatience with sexual euphemism directly at Sargeson via a critique of his fictional dialogue between Yate and Samuel Butler—another colonial identity around whom suspicions of unspeakable relations with men unfailingly congeal—as if the writer was to be held to blame for the persistence and inescapability of homosexual closets.[10] Rather than settle the question of Yate's (or Sargeson's) sexual innocence or guilt, we might reflect on the interpretative distortions exposed in this protracted debate and the seeming impossibility of full and final disclosure in the case of sexual relations between men.

Sargeson argues that the anachronistic deployment of the modern term confuses our recovery of those earlier configurations of desire. "Nobody in the first half of last century," he asserts,

> thought in terms of "homosexuality." There was of course, according to the law, "the abominable crime," punishable by death; but this seriously viewed felony was not, I think, particularly thought of as an affair of males since it could involve a male and a female, even a husband and

[9] On the operations of the closet, see Eve Kosofsky Sedgwick, *Epistemology of the Closet* (Berkeley: University of California Press, 1990).

[10] Kendrick Smithyman, review of *An Account of New Zealand and of the Formation and Progress of the Church Missionary Society's Mission in the Northern Island*, by William Yate, *Journal of the Polynesian Society* 82, no. 4 (1973): 436. Consider as well Kai Jensen's recent essay on Sargeson, which rescues the writer from the critical closet only to smother his homosexuality all the more effectively in hermeneutic banality. Jensen reads the male relations represented in Sargeson's fictions in terms of a homosexual subtext that is no longer legible so much as ubiquitous. Jensen, "Frank at Last," in *Opening the Book: New Essays on New Zealand Writers*, ed. Mark Williams and Michele Leggott (Auckland: Auckland University Press, 1995), 68–82. Michael King's biography, *Frank Sargeson: A Life* (Auckland: Viking, 1995), is sabotaged by a similar gay-friendly impulse: in his rush to accept Sargeson's sexual involvement with other men, King overlooks the specific social and literary consequences of the compulsory closeting of homosexuality.

wife (and in any case since the invention of the new word homosexuality, the abominable crime is seen not to be, strictly speaking, a homosexual act). But warm expressions of affection between people of the
same sex, provided there was discretion, no public indecency, and no
side-issues such as children or violence, were ignored by the law, and (as
we know from our literature as well as our historians), did not excite the
public interest nowadays so familiar to us.[11]

To judge that Yate was physically innocent of certain acts but emotionally guilty of a homosexual inclination is, therefore, to miss the
"nub of the matter" that "no charge could ever be brought against
Yate, because nobody had unequivocally alleged him to be guilty of
the abominable crime."[12] The substitution of *homosexual* for *sodomite* captures Yate for a modern understanding of sexuality conceived less as signature acts than as a holistic identity marked by
internal divisions and denials, by disavowed impulse and the thwarted
expression of an interior disposition. And as Sargeson parenthetically
points out, under this incoherent order it takes more—or in this case
less—than a certain sexual act to secure a sexuality. Sodomy within
the conjugal embrace fails to make either husband or wife a homosexual whereas crediting Yate with an emotional inclination un-
blunted by physicality nails the missionary to a now familiar sexual
cross: repression.

Sargeson's own assessment of Yate's career avoids anything resem-
bling a diagnostic summary, preferring to restore him to the ambiguous dispensations that sheltered him during his time among the Maori:

So Dr Binney's physical act and Mr Taylor's grossest indecency of character boil down to the endearing fondlings which Mr Yate without much
doubt bestowed upon the Maoris whom he much loved, and by whom
(as is clear from their letters), he was himself much loved. He writes in
his book of their ready affection, tears of farewell and smothering kisses.
"A New Zealander's love is all outside: it is in his eyes and his mouth,"
as he says they told him.[13]

This is to maintain rather than dispel the definitional opacity that

<hr>

[11] Sargeson, review of *Account of New Zealand*, 303.
[12] Sargeson, review of *Account of New Zealand*, 303.
[13] Sargeson, review of *Account of New Zealand*, 303.

clouds Yate's conduct from the contemporary gaze. Sargeson confounds or blurs the border between the man and his text and finally substitutes fulsome native avowal for European reticence. Such overlapping coincidences, and the interpretative effects generated though them, are endemic to the discourses that cohere around discussion of Yate's downfall. It is as though a male body, once pinioned by sexual suspicion, inevitably draws those who surround it into vertiginous spirals of interpretation.

Revision and Repetition

The question of Yate's ruin was taken up again by Binney, who some years later published an article in which she revised her reading of Yate in the light of further examination of the documents pertaining to his case. Her renewed investigations of the depositions and findings gathered in New Zealand against him prompts her to some startling retractions and reversals. Prior meditations on Yate's thwarted emotionality are swept aside in the face of new evidence that the missionary did engage in physical acts with other men. Binney's renewed inquiry turned up "notes" that suggest accusations were made which connected Yate with another of the *Prince Regent*'s crew, an ordinary seaman "improbably called Dick Deck."[14] Compiled from statements taken from passengers and seamen aboard the *Prince Regent*, the notes record "that there was an unbecoming intimacy between Mr Yate & Dennison [*sic*] considering their disparity of rank & education & moral deportment in as much as Mr Taylor has observed them tickle each other in passing & catch hold of each others legs these observations apply to Dick [crossed out] Deck as well as Dennison." These observations of physical and social familiarity are confirmed by the statements of other passengers, but the only explicitly indecent scenario recorded is from Taylor, who recalls "going down into Denison's Cabin Deck or Dennison drew a Curtain aside showing a naked female figure observed 'You see as we can't have the reality we must content

---

[14] The name, at least, has an allegorical appeal and seems to offer itself as a convenient midpoint on imperialism's erotic ladder, marking some level between the officer and the native. Judith Binney, "Whatever Happened to Poor Mr. Yate? An Exercise in Voyeurism," *New Zealand Journal of History* 9, no. 2 (1975): 117 and 124 n. 44.

ourselves with the likeness'—Mr Yate then lying on Denison's bed laughed & gave Dennison a slight pat on the head without reproving him." The more suggestive the notes, the more elliptical and syntactically elastic they become: "the chief officer even heard indecent conduct between Yate and the 3 mate 3mate and Yate lay together in the same berth . . . that Mr yate had been guilty of very indecent laughter with Mr Dennison—the 3 mate and Y had slept together at Mr Yates lodging—slept together at Mr Marsdens & had been observed with hands clasped under table and eyes locked had taken pieces of meat off plate That Mr Yate confirmed these reports X . . . Heard several reports from NZd—."[15]

Given the inconclusive content of the notes, Binney's attention is more focused on documents collected in New Zealand which refer to intimacies between Yate and the "Native Boys" at the Waimate mission, encounters that cannot be construed as other than sexual. This second set of statements is taken from some of the youths involved, all of whom lived as part of the mission population, taking lessons at the "Native Boys' School" in preparation for leading mission schools for Maori.[16] The four affidavits referred to by Binney are sworn and translated before the missionaries Richard Davis, William Williams, and George Clarke. In one, Toataua recounts several encounters with Yate, all of which occurred while the two were traveling together between mission stations:

> We arrived at Puriri. I slept in the tent of W. Yate we slept together. He said to me, Cast off your garments, I went and slept under his clothes. He said to me, Take hold of my penis. He laid upon me and __ with his hand and with my hand. __ __ We slept till break of day. In the morning he began again that work. ___ ___ I said to him, I am going out. He said to me I will flog you on the back. I was going outside. He laid hold of me and dragged me by my hand into the tent, and we titoitoi. That ended there. I went outside and he gave me one pound of tobacco as a payment.[17]

---

[15] I quote from statements held in the Mitchell Library, State Library of New South Wales, Sydney, among the William Colenso Papers, I, 1836–1899, A236, CY Reel 283, frames 414–22.

[16] For Yate's description of the several mission schools, see *Account of New Zealand*, 182–83.

[17] Deposition of Toataua. I quote directly from the depositions that are held to-

The other three deponents also swore that mutual masturbation, *kia tītoitoi tāua,* had occurred.[18] Samuel Kohe's statement tells of Yate taking him to his upstairs bedroom in Clarke's house to show him a picture of his sister, whom he suggests as a bride for Kohe before urging the young man to remove his clothes: "I said to him, For what purpose? He said to me that we may copulate. I replied, I do not understand what you are going to do. He said to me, All Europeans act thus while they are single men. Then because they sleep with their wives this practise is left off. But as for me my wife is this, a hand." Sex does not occur on this occasion, but Kohe goes on to testify that he and Yate masturbated together three times before his baptism, and "since my baptism I have been many times, more than I can count."[19] Philip Tohi also claims to have lost count of the number of times he and Yate have lain together with each taking hold of the other's penis. The deposition of Pehi frankly confirms similar activities and others that test the discretion of the European translators, who, confronted with vernacular description, resort to Latin: "Once at Pateretere, when we went to bathe. . . . He pulled off his trousers. He called to me, Come down into the water, I'll break your head with my penis. The deposition then goes on to state that he, W. Yate had a venereal connexion with the deponent, peni in ore imposito, promising to give him a pound of tobacco."

When faced with such submissions, the New Zealand missionaries, who had previously regarded "hints . . . dropped among the natives affecting Mr Yates moral character" as evidence of their tendency to "blaspheme," swept aside all skepticism. The depositions, Clarke claims, "have elicited facts which place it beyond the probability of a doubt that Mr Yate was during his residence in this land habitually guilty to an awful extent of the crime alluded to [in] Rom. 1.27 a body

gether in the Archives Office of New South Wales, Sydney, among the papers of the New South Wales colonial secretary. They form an enclosure in a letter from N.S.W. Crown Solicitor to N.S.W. Colonial Secretary, dated 12 December 1836. See 36/10481 in file 4/2357.1, Colonial Secretary, Letters Received, 1837.

[18] The Maori expression, shortened by Toataua to *tītoitoi,* is used in all four depositions with a parenthetical translation provided in Pehi's: "The meaning of this expression is, an act of most gross obscenity committed upon one another, each holding the penis of the other in his hand."

[19] Deposition of Samuel Kohe. Yate lived with the Clarkes first at Kerikeri, then at Waimate, where his bedroom was located on the ground floor of the house. Kohe's statement refers therefore to events before the founding of the Waimate station in 1830.

of evidence has been brought forward so circumstantial and so uniformly consistent as to leave no room for the shadow of a doubt."[20]
The biblical text was familiar to all the mission residents—Yate had
overseen the translation of this particular Scripture and its printing in
Maori sometime in 1832 or 1833. The missionary response to the witness of these young men was, however, generally Old Testament in
cast: the shadow of ignorance, once lifted, revealed the workings of divine retribution. James Busby, the British Resident in New Zealand,
writing to Governor Bourke's administration in New South Wales,
comments that God's wrath had been reflected in an alarming rise in
Maori mortality and cites biblical precedent. Once these despised
events were known, he continues, "in all the stations a day was appointed for humiliation and prayer for deliverance from the 'accursed
thing' and the part of the House which the unhappy man occupied was
with all his property and his horse burnt in a spot, which will hereafter be regarded I have no doubt as was the dead Sea which covered
offenders in the like kind of old."[21]

However, though God's wrath was said to have fallen among the native population and Yate's belongings unto his very horse were made
available for disciplinary spectacle, the sinful man proved beyond the
reach of human law. Busby goes on to write:

> There is one remarkable point which you ought to be made acquainted
> with, and which it is possible the Devil may have made a means of
> persuading the unhappy man that he was not sinning to the full extent
> of the crime which human laws have made penal & which called down
> in times of old the divine wrath. It is this. That it did not take place
> *per anum*—but it would appear merely by the instrumentality of the
> thighs.[22]

---

[20] Letter from George Clarke to parent committee of Church Missionary Society,
London, 28 September 1836, duplicate sent to Samuel Marsden, 4 November 1836,
Colonial Secretary, Letters Received 1837, 36/10480 in 4/2357.1.

[21] Letter from James Busby, British Resident at New Zealand, to T. C. Harington,
Esq., Colonial Secretary's Office, N.S.W., 15 November 1836, Colonial Secretary, Letters Received 1837, 4/2357.1. As frequently cited as it is, Busby's account is contra-
dicted by at least the Historic Places Trust of New Zealand, which is confident in the
curatorial identification of Yate's bedroom and study in the east wing of Clarke's residence at Waimate, now a museum.

[22] Letter from Busby to Harington, 15 November 1836.

December correspondence between the crown solicitor's and colonial secretary's offices confirms the legal opinion that on the basis of the depositions, "the crime of Sodomy cannot be proved."[23] Francis Fisher, crown solicitor, advises that unless Busby can "distinctly ascertain the facts of time, place, & under what circumstance the crime was committed—& unless it clearly can be proved that the offence was committed per anum, the capital part of the charge will fail." Should Busby be unable to secure such evidence, then there is "no adequate means by which in law this wretched criminal can be punished and in such case," writes Fisher, "I apprehend His Excellency [Governor Bourke] will rather allow the Individual to escape even the slight punishment which might [likely] be inflicted for the misdemeanour than expose the enormity of his offence by giving Evidence of facts which cannot be met with a sentence equal to the depravity they disclose."[24]

The information turned up in the archives seems to return to and confirm Sargeson's point that in the early part of the nineteenth century accusations of misconduct between males stand or fall on the disputation of sodomy. But there is no need to hurry that conclusion; it is almost the least interesting thing uncovered here. In the face of the new revelations, sodomy starts to look like a safe place, a legal loophole or point of law that offers containment where those other more mobile activities or pleasures that press into the representational foreground of the depositions seem always to require deflective translation—into Maori, into Latin—or prompt still more exegetical departure and doubling. In the 1970s, no less than in the 1830s, effects are generated around an imagined sexual connection between men, and further, the stumbling self-correcting entry into historical scholarship seems doomed to repeat the foreclosure of the initial inquiry. The moment at which the Church Missionary Society hierarchy abandoned the inquiry into Yate's behavior was when it recognized that the relations described in the affidavits were not forensically sodomitical.

Binney, moreover, finds herself in a related interpretative cul-de-sac as she is forced to conclude that Yate's sustained attempt to have the allegations against him heard in court indicates that he too knew his invulnerability to the letter of this law. This is to attribute a cynicism

[23] Letter from Francis Fisher, Crown Solicitor, to the Colonial Secretary, 12 December 1836, Colonial Secretary, Letters Received 1837, 36/736 in file 4/2357.1.

[24] Letter from Francis Fisher, Crown Solicitor, to the Colonial Secretary, also dated 12 December 1836, Colonial Secretary, Letters Received 1837, 36/735 in file 4/2357.1.

to Yate in these matters, although that suggestion is more properly directed at the agencies that refused to convene a court in which to try him. After all, in the eighteenth and nineteenth centuries accusations of sodomitical behavior tended to circulate inside courtrooms in the context of defamation suits. That is, it was not generally the case that courts were convened to try men for sodomy but that men so slandered called courts to try their accusers. When courts were called to try sodomy, they were often courts-martial, and as Arthur Gilbert's work on the Royal Navy reveals, such courts frequently retreated behind the exactness of the legal prohibition, which required evidence of seminal emission *in anum,* in their reluctance to convict men of this capital offense.[25] Exceptions to this rule tended to occur in times of war or mutiny when the ban on sodomy became the most convenient way of policing other, treasonable acts. In this context it might be supposed that the sodomitical suspicions falling on Yate could have been an effective means for the Church Missionary Society to discipline him for other professional misdemeanors less easy to police: his leaving for England in 1894 without permission, his publishing *An Account of New Zealand* without the knowledge or consent of his peers, and his raising of English funds for the church at Waimate against the will of both the missionary society and the settlers.[26]

There is, however, another way of reading what is at stake in the repeated abuse of Yate. Although the Church Missionary Society members accept the evidence against Yate amassed in New Zealand and so judge that the couplings described in the affidavits did occur, they all seem singularly uninterested in those embraces. The same might be said of Binney's reconstruction of events. Neither the missionaries nor the historian spends any time in imagining those sexual encounters, in giving them any social or erotic profile. It might be helpful, therefore, to suspend the impulse to convict or acquit Yate and take the time to elaborate the shape those pleasures might have taken in the minds of Yate's contemporaries whether or not they did transpire.

[25] See Arthur N. Gilbert, "The *Africaine* Courts Martial: A Study of Buggery and the Royal Navy," *Journal of Homosexuality* 1 (1974): 111–22, and "Buggery and the British Navy, 1700–1861," *Journal of Social History* 10 (1976): 72–98.

[26] For more on Yate's nonsexual transgressions and his general unpopularity, see Judith Binney, "William Yate," in *The Dictionary of New Zealand Biography,* Volume 1: *1769–1869,* ed. W. H. Oliver (Wellington: Allen and Unwin for the Department of Internal Affairs, 1990), 611–12.

Conversion

As Binney informs us, in the process of investigating Yate's conduct and of securing the affidavits from Pehi, Toataua, and the others, the New Zealand missionaries are convinced

> that these practices of Yate's, together with the habit bordering on prostitution, of paying for them with gifts, had been a common occurrence with a number of young men. James Busby, citing their enquiries, talked of sixty or more—but added, hesitantly, that being rather deaf and apt to mishear numbers, he must surely be incorrect. But he may not have been, as, according to William Williams' reckoning sent to Marsden in November 1836, "no less than 50 Natives . . . have been with him, and I doubt not but there are not fewer than 100."[27]

In these accounts the numbers keep multiplying. It seems the easiest thing in the world for these men of God to imagine that Yate had shared sexual intimacies with each and every mission boy. Samuel Marsden bluntly declared that he "had no doubt of [Yate's] Guilt from the first moment I was informed of his Conduct—and no one could Change my mind" and, though infirm, sailed from his home in New South Wales to the Bay of Islands, where he could investigate matters first hand.[28] Marsden, like Williams, had no difficulty assuming that Yate had enjoyed immoral connection with all his Maori charges. Both men believed that the private scenes of instruction Yate shared with young Maori men in preparation for their conversion to the Christian faith were inevitably marked by such pleasures. Clarke was appalled by precisely this coincidence between catechism and persuasion to obscenity:

> The following general facts have been elicited, viz., that the abominable practices of [Yate] began soon after he came to the land. That every station in which he resided has been polluted by them. That they were car-

---

[27] Binney, "Poor Mr. Yate," 114–15.

[28] Letter from Samuel Marsden to New Zealand missionaries, 19 December 1836, Marsden Papers II, A1993, 123, Mitchell Library, State Library of New South Wales, Sydney. Marsden's twisted investment in the Yate affair and his obsessive desire to uncover corruption at first hand can be gleaned from the very differing accounts of the scandal in Eric Ramsden, *Marsden and the Missions: Prelude to Waitangi* (Sydney: Angus and Robertson, 1936), 20–44, and Bill Wannan, *Very Strange Tales: The Turbulent Times of Samuel Marsden* (Melbourne: Lansdowne Press, 1962), 163–69.

ried on at the native villages which he visited and even in the road to
those villages and shocking to state that he introduced to christian Baptism the very natives, who both before and afterwards were the mis-
guided partakers in his guilt. In short we are overwhelmed with grief at
the [reflection] of the extent of evil carried among the different tribes
which he was accustomed to visit professedly to impart religious instruction.[29]

Conversion by Yate in these contemporaneous accounts is always a
double seduction, and the success of Yate's method—to which the letters published by him as part of *An Account of New Zealand* are said
to bear eloquent witness—smuggles in the suggestion that sexual congress slickened his recruitment drive: who better to further an evan-
gelical dream conceived as the initiation of the heathen subject into
the knowledge of sin?

Binney's discussion of these letters tends to repeat this peculiar interpretative effect. The evangelist's "emotionalism" converts others
to its cause precisely because it maps onto a native difference: the
Christian magnification of sin and depravity finds itself at home in a
culture "without inhibition." The letters

> all expose the concentration of his teachings on sin. They also reveal the
> particular attachment of his pupils for him. These letters, more than
> Yate's own writings, reveal the dilemma of the missionary vulnerable to
> sensuality. Yate transferred to his pupils the idea of the need first to
> awaken to the perils of the unregenerate soul and the carnal energies of
> man. He instigated among them a practice of writing zealous letters to
> himself . . . all of which are emotionally very highly charged.[30]

The letters written to Yate by his Maori converts are certainly unique,
freighted as they are with a kind of doubled awkwardness, that of
Christian catechism certainly but also of the epistolary posture itself:
"Sir, how do you do? this is my speech to you. The sacred day was the
day in which this book was written. . . . Listen to this my speech to
you. How do you do, Mr. Yate? This book is words about nothing; it
is my lips which speak to you: perhaps it is not my heart; perhaps it

---

[29] Letter from Clarke, 28 September 1836.
[30] Binney, "Poor Mr. Yate," 113.

is my lips only. This is all my speech to you; mine."[31] Although Yate includes these letters in his book to testify to the wonders of native conversion and Binney sees in them evidence of Yate's correspondents' "highly charged" emotional regard for him, I cannot help but read them as energized by nothing so much as a frenzied joy in being letter writers at last, as fascinated by the material processes as by the transactional effects of writing. "This is all my book to you," writes another to Yate, "this is all my writing, mine, the son of TEMORENGA, sitting in the verandah of his house at Manawenua. Perhaps you can read this book—perhaps not. Bad are my fingers for writing, mine."[32]

Once suspicion falls on Yate's conduct, it seems his methods are infallible. This duality plagues the representation of Yate's vocation. William Williams was distressed precisely "because the young men involved were credible witnesses, being of 'good character,' many of them now baptised members of the new church who 'were seduced into this vice in the days of their ignorance.'"[33] Yate, with his knowledge of Maori and Latin, *kia tītoitoi tāua* and fellatio, operated under several incoherent dispensations: he was less a disobedient missionary than an exemplary one. Foucault, for one, might have predicted that Yate's activities would remain strategically integral to the formative disciplining of first native and then European subjects, comprising an "especially dense transfer point for relations of power" that are untroubled by seeming contradictions. The discourses of sexuality that will congeal around activities such as those connecting Yate and his Christian boys are far from "intractable" but are rather "endowed with the greatest instrumentality: useful for the greatest number of maneuvres and capable of serving as a point of support, as a linchpin, for the most varied strategies."[34] Christian pedagogy has it both ways, being fueled by impulses it can simultaneously deny, stigmatize, or reject. The intensity of the language of the *Account of New Zealand* and of that employed by the Maori candidates in their letters to Yate derives from Scripture and insistently invokes broadly erotic

[31] William Marshall Hau, in *An Account of New Zealand,* by William Yate, 280–81.

[32] The son of Temorenga, in *An Account of New Zealand,* by William Yate, 263.

[33] Quoted in Binney, "Poor Mr. Yate," 115.

[34] Michel Foucault, *The History of Sexuality,* vol. 1: *An Introduction,* trans. Robert Hurley (New York: Pantheon, 1978), 103.

possibilities that would be violently repudiated in other contexts.[35] It is that contradiction which is unleashed when the four converted speak of Yate's love and their love for him in forms of legal testimony.

Community

One of the critical effects of the refusal to consider the nature of the transactions described in the sworn depositions of the Maori youths is the continued sequestering of the mission residents into separate populations: European and Maori. The missionary Davis was the only one who, when reflecting on Yate's conduct, spoke of such acts being familiar to Maori rather than something unknown he had communicated to them.[36] To most of Yate's brethren, however, the grapplings of Yate and the Maori youths were strangely transient; they did not outlast their moment or his presence in the colony. The missionaries did not pursue the alleged sins as they may have reverberated among the native population. The young men involved—four, sixty, or one hundred of them—were not considered marked by that crime, which was itself erased with the burning of Yate's belongings and the shooting of his horse. There is, perhaps, something in the exemption of the Maori from blame and in the spectacular eradication won by the firing of Yate's possessions which suggests the peculiar contours of the missionary understanding of his fall. Yate's sexual sins were figured not as crimes against the Maori but as crimes against his own community.

According to the journal of the Reverend Taylor—one of the two men who first drew official scrutiny to Yate—the New Zealand missionaries, having unveiled the deeds perpetrated in their midst, deemed Waimate, the site of Yate's residence, "the Vale of Achan."[37]

[35] On the similarly impassioned discourses of New English Puritanism and their violent, equivocal deployments of an eroticized homosociality, see Michael Warner, "New English Sodom," *American Literature* 64, no. 1 (1992): 19–47.

[36] See Binney, "Poor Mr. Yate," 115. Compare Busby's lament: "What a proof of the desperate depravity of the human heart—I understand that he is ascertained to have made not fewer than 60 persons the Instruments of his unnatural lust—and it is to be feared has added to the Catalogue of their former Crimes this worst of all, which was never before heard of amongst the natives." Letter from Busby to Harington, 15 November 1836.

[37] The reference to Taylor's journal entry of 13 December 1836 is given in Binney,

When they thought of Yate and gave his unspeakable crimes a communicable form, the New Zealand missionaries invoked the Old Testament example of Achan, whose story is told in the Book of Joshua. Achan, in defiance of a command from Joshua, took of the spoil from Jericho and hid in his tent that which had been reserved exclusively for God. Achan did not confess his theft until Joshua, having cast lots, confronted him. Achan's subsequent admission of guilt gained him a place in the world to come, though his sin cost him his life and he and all his extended family were stoned, their possessions and the devoted goods from the fallen city burned alongside them, such punishment being exacted in the Valley of Achor. As most commentary on these verses underlines, Achan's crime was the first act of disobedience after the tribes of Israel crossed the Jordan, his death the first divinely commanded punishment in the new land. The story stands, therefore, as evidence of the Israelite conception of the need for solidarity within a perilous collectivity that is always threatened from without. Until the thief was detected, the Israelites were unfavored by God, being defeated at Ai. Thus the sin of one was imputed to the entire community, and by the same rule Achan's family and his goods had to perish with him at the appointed place of punishment, which then took his name, Achor.

Exegetically enlarged, the Book of Joshua provides a means of interpreting events in Waimate after the disclosure of Yate's covetous acts. When Joshua, by divine sleuthing, detected the sinner among the tribes of Israel, his discovery led to an act of extreme social consolidation in the new land. It was not an act against an alien people, such as the sacking of Jericho, but the violent sacrifice of the alien within— the eradication of all trace of Achan and his kind. The wide cast of the purge confirms that Achan's sin was against his community as much as it was against his God. This is a chilling text through which to read

introduction to *Account of New Zealand*, xvii n. 41. The account of this day that Ramsden provides likewise privileges this understanding of Yate's sin and the scene of its unfolding through the invocation of biblical precedent: "When Marsden visited New Zealand the following year he discovered instance after instance of Yate's misconduct. Taylor declared that the former had the confessions of six of Yate's 'deluded victims.' The missionaries said they could send at least one hundred more. To 'avert the wrath of an offended God' they kept a day of solemn fast and humiliation. Yate's property was burnt by his former colleagues: they even shot his inoffensive horse. Then, before returning to their homes they conferred upon the scene of William Yate's labours the title of 'Vale of Achan.'" Ramsden, *Marsden and the Missions*, 36.

the actions of the New Zealand missionaries. It is as though Yate's sin-
ning with other men is the crime the mission had been waiting to de-
tect, the crime involving a Christian man that required the staging of
a spectacle of expulsion and eradication. The consolidation of the
Christian collectivity in the new land waits on this particular sexual
sin, the detection of which cleanses the ranks of the Waimate mission
and made of its members proto–New Zealanders.

The policing and reviling of these stigmatized acts assists in defining the community, and further the nation, by establishing everything
they are not. Yate's sin may well have been the sin of location, there
being a long-held tradition that invests sexual relations between men
with significance to the social body and its implied geographies. "At
however fantasmatic a level," Michael Warner notes, the very term
sodomy, like its counterpart, *lesbianism*, suggests "a map of sexual
knowledges and exotic origins. No other terms in the language of sexuality have a comparable etymology, as though unlike all other sexual
acts—if they even *are* acts—these two were practiced not by individuals but by cities, islands, or nations."[38] This logic of metonymic contagion is traceable in the way the crimes alleged of Yate cast a shadow
on the place in which they were said to occur. In the biblical text invoked as gloss on Yate's actions, Joshua declared that Achan had troubled Israel and that God would trouble him. The site of his execution
was known therefore as "trouble" (in Hebrew *akor*), and the wordplay
is developed in Chronicles, where Achan's name is rendered "Achar."
The Reverend Taylor's phrase, "the Vale of Achan," serves the same
metaphorical compression: the man of trouble bestows his name on
the place of trouble, with which he is indistinguishable. Waimate is the
troubled place, and Yate's sin becomes the occasion for settlement. As
in Joshua the sin is eclipsed by its detection and punishment, which
double motion enacts its placement and secures the arrival of the community in the new land: the inflamed place is now marked as theirs.

The way Marsden, Taylor, Williams, and the mission brethren
availed themselves of the pleasures Yate was alleged to have taken
with Maori men partakes of a particular kind of cultural fantasy. Its
frenzy is spent to effect an exemplary disciplining of the collective,

[38] Warner, "New English Sodom," 21. According to Warner, this "hidden fantasy
about the geography of sex" continues to be manifested in the still current "assumption that sodomitical and lesbian sex are more germane to public politics than other
kinds of sex" (ibid.).

though its violence is only and always directed at specific bodies, at men like Yate, and in his absence, his horse. If the missionary imagination detects and punishes the sexual sin between men to ensure the survival of the community in its new home, then the legacy of the Church Missionary Society may be that godliness and then nationhood are made dependent on the erasure of this difference within, perhaps especially as that difference can be made to map onto a native similitude. These practices, as Taylor admitted, were not unknown to the Maori.

Yate was not the first sinner among the Church Missionary Society in the Bay of Islands—some ten years earlier Thomas Kendall had fallen into adultery with a Maori girl of seventeen, and Kendall's successor had lapses into drunkenness—but although these failings caused the mission more than a little embarrassment, they did not occasion the vehement repudiation that was given over to Yate's sin, the day dedicated to erasing what remained of him among them. The repudiation of Yate, unlike that of Kendall, say, marks the community's arrival in this place; it was the necessary expulsion that symbolically enacted their occupation of this space as their own. As guilty as Kendall is, his heterosexually inflected sins are fully retrievable for a later colonial logic. In Binney's biography of Kendall the adulterous missionary is captured for liberal appropriation, his sexual fall read as a descent into self-knowledge and the complications of colonial history.[39] Kendall's sexual sin may become the sign of his empathetic crossing over to the Maori, but this romanticism makes no purchase on Yate's errancy. If Binney's first essay respects only the latency of the emotional homosexual, bestowing a morality on Yate's celibacy, her second, composed in the light of the affidavits, abandons him to a sad, lonely, ultimately tormented fate.[40]

The crimes alleged of Yate might, however, be available to alternative imaginings, replayed as often in our minds as in, say, Marsden's and thus recovered for other historical projects. Those acts—furtive

---

[39] Judith Binney, *The Legacy of Guilt: A Life of Thomas Kendall* (Auckland: Oxford University Press, 1968).

[40] "If we can finally end the whole sad tale of William Yate, it is to say that he was not the victim of a false scandal and colonial gossip-mongering. . . . Yate's tragedy lies, not so much in his persecution, as a man who was technically innocent yet morally guilty, but in the torment of mind he must have undergone in reconciling his desires with his Christian morality." Binney, "Poor Mr. Yate," 122.

or sweet, with whatever degree of mutuality, coercion, or shared vulnerability we bestow on them—can be made to speak the possibilities of encounter as well as its abuses. The missionaries secure the solidarity of their ministry with the expulsion of sodomitical dissonance, but the discursive technologies of detection and expulsion are not foolproof. The fall of William Yate, the strange thought of sexual connection between men at a mission station, might also open a rift, revealing the instabilities that mine the imagined community, calling into doubt the boundaries and exclusions the community assumes. The adjacency of disparate codes of sexual conduct between Maori and European at this moment of Pacific settlement forces into discourse— both the lucid affidavits as well as the more tortured syntax of the records of the colonial and church administration—conflations of sexual understanding that are unimaginable elsewhere.[41]

Bust

Sargeson had more reason than most to distrust notions of commonality based on the denial of difference and to be concerned by the fate of Yate. Born Norris Davey, he was as a young man the churchly type, still an active member of Hamilton's Methodist Young Men's Bible class into his twenties. In Wellington in September 1929, when he was twenty-seven years old, he met an older man in a public place and was invited to return to his rented room. He went and "later in the evening, when the two men were masturbating each other, . . . detectives forced their way into the room and arrested them both for indecent assault."[42] Though found guilty, Davey escaped the punishment of the law by deflecting it toward his sexual partner; under the

---

[41] In the wake of Benedict Anderson, *Imagined Communities: Reflections on the Origin and Spread of Nationalism* (London: Verso, 1983), and George Mosse, *Nationalism and Sexuality* (Madison: University of Wisconsin Press, 1985), much has been written about the denials enforced in the name of an imagined community. Sedgwick reminds us, however, that we cannot know in advance how those two terms, nationalism and sexuality, might destabilize each other. Eve Kosofsky Sedgwick, "Nationalisms and Sexualities in the Age of Wilde," in *Nationalisms and Sexualities*, ed. Andrew Parker, Mary Russo, Doris Sommer, and Patricia Yaeger (New York: Routledge, 1992), 235–45. This insight provides a suggestive bridge between the affairs of Yate and the role of the gay Sargeson in founding a canon of national literature.

[42] King, *Frank Sargeson*, 93.

direction of his counsel he posed as the victim of the other man's persuasion and testified against him. Sargeson's biographer, Michael King, provides one way of reading Davey's entrapment: "After accepting privately for at least three years that he was homosexual," the young man was "forced to deny this aspect of his nature and identity, to act as if it was the abomination society believed it to be, to give evidence against a fellow homosexual who had wished him no harm, and to testify that he would never again participate in such activities."[43] In the courtroom, according to King, Davey repudiated the sexuality abhorrent to the state and so avoided imprisonment; he made his escape to the hospitable ground of his uncle's farm, where he reinvented himself as the sexually dissident writer, Frank Sargeson, whose prototype New Zealand fictions inscribe multiple pathways of male identification. Yet this version of things, though it has its consolations, neglects to address the way the space of writing is continuous with the juridical space of the courtroom. Sargeson's literary discourse—strangely graphic stories that are as perversely national as they are sexual—is as adept at staging elaborate rituals of erasure as the discourse of police entrapment, which he is said to have turned his back on.[44] Both represent, to very different ends, a homosexuality known and cultivated though readily denied.

On Yate's final return to England, he, his sister Sarah, and Denison, the third officer of the *Prince Regent*, on whom his immoral attentions were said to have focused, took up house together, though we have no way of knowing the private cast of that domestic arrangement.[45]

---

[43] King, *Frank Sargeson*, 95.

[44] A more suggestive approach to Sargeson's literary strategies and alibis might consider his writing in relation to that of his contemporaries E. H. McCormick and Bill Pearson, whose contributions to Pacific studies have yet to be recognized as other than straight. In particular, Pearson's *Rifled Sanctuaries: Some Views of the Pacific Islands in Western Literature to 1900* (Auckland: Auckland University Press, 1984) finds in the pages of Pacific literature many stranded men whose island existence "involves an ambivalence or watchfulness" that marks the very limits of their culture (61). Neither one thing nor the other, the difficult territory these figures occupy may be analogous to the situation of the hero of Pearson's novel, *Coal Flat* (1963), whom he described in 1990 as "a man who has hardly admitted to himself that he is a homosexual." See Pearson's autobiographical piece, "Beginnings and Endings," in which he considers the evolution of *Coal Flat* and its inscription of a homosexual theme necessarily carried by a heterosexual plot. Pearson, "Beginnings and Endings," *Sport* 5 (1990): 16–17.

[45] See Binney, "Poor Mr. Yate," 124 n. 39.

Thwarted by the refusal of the Church Missionary Society to investigate his case despite his pamphlets and the intervention of influential gentlemen on his behalf, Yate was banned from taking any permanent position as a clergyman. It was not until 1846, under powerful patronage, that he was able to take up employment as a chaplain to an abandoned chapel for seamen in Dover, where he worked among sailors until his death some thirty years later.[46] The felicity of Yate's final appointment to the Mission for Seamen would not have been lost on Sargeson, many of his own fictions transpiring in similar, admittedly seedier, locations: doss houses, hotel bars, detention cells. The Sailor's Home at Dover might have seemed to him another of those male institutions through which a fundamentally homosocial culture regulates relations between men, thereby seeming to sanction the recognitions and initiations—the avuncular devotions—that it simultaneously disavows.

This chapter has relocated the fall of Yate, its documentary sources and scholarly interpretations, within a larger argument about the continued significance of same-sex sexual possibility in national discourses, particularly those that have emerged in the postcolonial Pacific. Sargeson's fictions have always been recognized as central to the emergence of New Zealand literary identity, although the role of male-male sexuality in establishing that national identity generates as much ambivalence now as it did in the early mission fields of the far north. Despite the continued ambivalence generated likewise around the sexual actions of Yate, we cannot afford to misrecognize his part in New Zealand's colonial legacy. As events in Waimate testify, the distinctive quality of Pacific encounter yields a modern sexuality that is not reducible to either European or indigenous sexual norms but the result of a reciprocal evolution of European and Pacific sexual practices engaged in the colonial context.

[46] Binney, introduction to *Account of New Zealand*, xx.

5   Gauguin's *Manao Tupapau* and Sodomitical Invitation

Ambivalence has become a crucial term in analyses of colonial discourse that stress not the univocal nature of imperial power but its fraught internal divisions and the dialectical relationships that mesh together colonial agents and subjects in unstable cross-identifications. The readings that make up this book themselves rely on ambivalence to designate a space of incoherence that might be found in each of the South Pacific texts discussed so far: Cook's voyage, Melville's narrative, and Yate's career. In each reading the term *ambivalence* gathers to itself not one but two privileged adjectives: colonial and sexual. This book suggests not that ambivalence is the limit point of imperialism, its weak spot or sign of failure, but that ambivalence better designates the facility of imperial power to reinvent itself in strategic response to a range of locally specific triggers. In the case of William Yate, for instance, his sexual interactions with the native population, once uncovered, did not weaken the authority of the Church Missionary Society but further legitimated its hegemonic presence in New Zealand and reinvigorated its interventions in indigenous practices that could be understood as abusive.[1] The discipli-

---

[1] Nicholas Thomas identifies the way "popular missionary works on Pacific societies" provided a "negative image" of indigenous practices, particularly those involving inequalities of gender, so that "Christianity can thus be seen as a liberating and reforming social force, as well as a spiritually enlightening one." *Marquesan Societies: Inequality and Political Transformation in Eastern Polynesia* (Oxford: Clarendon Press, 1990), 62.

nary effects of this response to sexual scandal were not, however, limited to Yate, or to the boys who were his willing partners, but included in their target those who accused him as well. Sexual ambivalence is thus instrumental to the operation of a colonial power, whose effects can never be confidently second-guessed.

This chapter inquires into the continued overlap between colonial ambivalence and sexual ambivalence as it has been assumed or argued in recent critical writing about Paul Gauguin's Pacific paintings. It examines how Gauguin's work is either taken as evidence of the way a heavily sexualized primitivism is continuous with colonialist paradigms of difference or alternately figured as the site of colonialism's most thoroughgoing critique. Gauguin's female nude of 1892, *Manao tupapau*, has become a cornerstone to both critical schools, which, in order to secure their counterposed arguments, interpret Gauguin's paintings in relation to, on the one hand, an overinvested distinction between masculinity and femininity and, on the other, a distinction between heterosexuality and homosexuality that is finally of no consequence. If the possibility of male–male sexual encounter seems not to have occurred to the first (putatively feminist) school of criticism, it is continually invoked by the second (psychoanalytic) school but only to newly invest heterosexuality with an ambivalence now considered foundational. It is the argument of this chapter that this second school of criticism can be shown to repeat the original gesture of Gauguin's painting, whereby the incorporation of homosexual possibility is deflected toward a heterosexual outcome that insofar as it now represents the thing that it is not, becomes all the more alluring. Sexual ambivalence, in both instances, is staged in relation to a same-sex sexual possibility the better to set that possibility aside.

Sadistic Gaze

Two recent and influential feminist discussions of Gauguin's Pacific oeuvre have no time for ambivalence when it comes to analyzing Gauguin's imbrication in the aesthetic practices and ruses of imperialism. Abigail Solomon-Godeau argues that Gauguin's primitivist representation of Polynesian women reveals a "gendered discourse" that is continuous with a colonialist "dynamic of knowledge/power relations which admits of no reciprocity" and which dates to the "expeditionary literature generated by Captain Cook, Wallis, Bougainville and the countless successive voyagers to the South Seas, [in which] the colonial encounter is first and foremost the encounter with the body of the Other."[2] Griselda Pollock likewise cites the work of Gauguin as supplying "the fantasy scenarios and the exotic *mise-en-scène* for not only masculinist but also imperialist narratives."[3] Both these critiques of Gauguin's primitivism target his preoccupation with the exotic female body and its availability for visualization, but the invocation of this "gendered discourse," founded as it is on a gaze that is both male—or phallic—and colonialist, obscures what I take to be the more unsettling recognition: the body that compels Gauguin's experiments in a Pacific primitivism is not that of the native woman but that of the European male crossed by his Polynesian counterpart. As overrepresented as the native female body is in Gauguin's Tahitian and Marquesan paintings, to continue to cede it interpretative priority as these recent readings do is, perhaps, to miss the peculiar vulnerabilities and denials staged in those paintings and to foreclose, in the name of gender, questions of sexuality.[4]

When Solomon-Godeau, in particular, invokes the male gaze, what is she referring to? In a review article on the troubled if ubiquitous importation of psychoanalytic theory into film and media studies, Craig Saper reminds us that the concept of the gaze, now indispensable to both feminist film theory and art criticism, was initially borrowed from psychoanalysis.[5] Saper notes that as the concept has passed between those disciplines, it has retained some familiar modifiers and picked up a few more. The gaze is frequently designated, or thought, phallic, patriarchal, male. His point is that such understandings of the visual and psychic dynamics of the gaze owe little to the Lacanian

<hr>

[2] Abigail Solomon-Godeau, "Going Native," *Art in America* 77, no. 7 (1989): 123–24.

[3] Griselda Pollock, *Avant-Garde Gambits, 1888–1893: Gender and the Colour of Art History* (London: Thames and Hudson, 1992), 8.

[4] Stephen F. Eisenman, in *Gauguin's Skirt* (London: Thames and Hudson, 1997), is similarly hesitant about the way both Pollock and Solomon-Godeau indict the artist for collaborating in "colonial ideologies of racism and sexism" (91). Eisenman wishes not to ignore these implications but to approach them from a perspective that acknowledges the possibility that those discourses might have encountered some resistance in the colonial theater.

[5] Craig Saper, "A Nervous Theory: The Troubling Gaze of Psychoanalysis in Media Studies," *Diacritics* 21, no. 4 (1991): 33–52.

analysis from which they are said to derive. At worst, this gendering of the gaze has reduced its analytic power to the formulaic "men gaze at women" or, more clunkily, "men as desiring subjects gaze at women as objects." These phrases, and the understandings of the gaze which they map, tend to be embedded in analyses of film or art that ascribe sadistic mastery to the agent that views and thereby collapse the operation of the gaze into that of vision. Such is the unacknowledged maneuver animating Solomon-Godeau's article on Gauguin, in which the artist deploys a demonized male gaze "implicated in fantasies of imaginary knowledge, power and rape." These fantasies, she insists, "are sometimes underpinned by real power, by real rape." Solomon-Godeau thus bestows on Gauguin a capacity for violence—both imaginary and real—that can never be mitigated by historical circumstance, only confirmed. The "primitivist artist," in this account, rather than implicated in the order of specularity, is its idealized agent, whose unassailable "psychic armature" has a "historic" counterpoint in imperial "relations of violence and domination."[6]

In art criticism this tendency to collapse the gaze into vision is exacerbated by the fact that its traditional theoretical lexicon has never quite escaped the anthropomorphic fallacy. Even in its more formalist moments art criticism appeals to the eye, so viewpoint implies viewer and even perspective usually belongs to, or outrages, someone. Rather than refer to this as the operation of the gaze, it would be useful to retain the term *look* for the kind of view that naturalizes itself, that asks that we accept it as sight, as proceeding from an individual's position. The look, then, is associated with the function of the eyes, and much feminist-inflected criticism continues to think of those eyes as lodged within the pleasured body of a spectator, the usual suspect being the male voyeur. In distinction to the look, the term *gaze* is reserved for the structural articulation of a scopic field that exceeds or disrupts the anthropomorphic ideal of vision. The gaze is an altogether more discontinuous notion than sight, deriving its representational functionality from relations of subjectification that are, at best, intermittently stabilized but never ended or entirely successful. In this sense the gaze frames or checks the fallacy of the look, suggesting its inability to reach or fully subjugate its object. The relation between these terms can be demonstrated in a reading of Gauguin's

---

[6] Solomon-Godeau, "Going Native," 125.

Manao tupapau, a painting in which the subject who looks is entangled in a gaze that exceeds the binary—and heterosexual—scopic paradigm that both Solomon-Godeau and Pollock rely on.

Retreat

The story of Gauguin's Pacific career, repeatedly retold as it is, is now recognized as the story of repetition itself. In 1901, ten years after his first arrival in Tahiti, a tired and jaded Gauguin, in a final attempt to elude civilization, sails to the rumoredly cannibal Marquesas. Dogged by ill health, Gauguin proceeds to build a studio that was a transposed and belated version of Te Faruru, the "Studio of the South Seas," he had created in Paris toward the end of 1893 on his return from Tahiti. The olive green and chrome yellow walls of Gauguin's metropolitan atelier had been hung with his unsold Tahitian paintings, and the light-flooded space also accommodated his sculpture, current work, and the ethnographic collection of his Uncle Zizi. There, among those artifacts and other "flea-market exotica," he held weekly soirées, where he lectured about method, told stories from his travels, and played music to his assembled guests.[7] Created eight years later, the Marquesan atelier, already a faded repetition, advertises primitivism and savagery in louder tones than its Parisian prototype. Gavan Daws describes what was to be Gauguin's final residence:

This time he identified his home in big characters carved into a wood panel over his lintel: *"Maison du Jouir,"* House of Pleasure, meaning sexual pleasure, perhaps a reference to the traditional sexual meeting houses of the old Polynesian culture, certainly a statement of personal appetite. On the walls were forty-five pornographic photographs bought at Port Said between France and the South Seas. . . . [Gauguin] went about the house naked, leaning on his walking sticks, the heads of which were carved to represent a phallus and a couple in sexual embrace. He acquired a dog and named it Pego, a version of the abbreviated signature he sometimes used on his paintings, "PGo," which when said aloud

[7] Richard Brettell, "The Return to France," in *The Art of Paul Gauguin*, ed. Richard Brettell, Françoise Cachin, Claire Frèches-Thory, and Charles F. Stuckey (Washington, D.C.: National Gallery of Art, 1988), 301.

sounded like sailor's slang for "penis." Every time Gauguin called his
dog he was being outrageous, and he knew it.[8]

Gauguin's career was often reduced to the serial indignity of the repeated restart, but the multiple arrivals and departures required by the
primitivist agenda are such that it becomes hard to keep relations of
priority and precedence stable. In this chronology the relation between original and copy seems finally replaced by a series of simula-
tions, like so many smutty postcards carried between metropolitan
center and colonial margin, in which all productions are restagings,
marked by a sense of belatedness and inauthenticity.

Christopher Bongie suggests that all exotic travelers find themselves, like Gauguin, in strained relation to time and space, their expectations of arrival forestalled by the spread of imperialism, so that
their savage destinations keep receding even as they approach.[9] By the
late nineteenth-century this experiential trajectory has been thoroughly routinized and commodified so that the aching nostalgia that
Bongie locates at the heart of the exotic enterprise maps seamlessly
with capitalism's touristic trajectory. As is well known, Gauguin's
own interest in Polynesia was inspired by the artificial villages and
huts displayed at the 1889 Universal Exhibition in Paris.[10] Once primitivism's exotic ambition is compromised by the global reach of capitalism, however, the voyage out, which was to have been a voyage
back, is more frequently figured as a voyage in, to the remote regions
of the self.

More recent, and more sympathetic, discussions of Gauguin take as
their subject the psychic trajectory of primitivism, which directs the
artist toward racial and sexual territory thought beyond the reach of
repression or civilized restraint. For these critics, the ambivalence
of the artist's interest in the native and the perverse returns as a kind
of psychic come-uppance, installing an insufficiency at the heart of

[8] Gavan Daws, *A Dream of Islands: Voyages of Self-Discovery in the South Seas*
(Milton, Queensland: Jacaranda Press, 1980), 261.

[9] Christopher Bongie, *Exotic Memories: Literature, Colonialism, and the Fin de
Siècle* (Stanford: Stanford University Press, 1991).

[10] Pollock takes this "tourist fantasy of the trip to the South Pacific" as further evidence of Gauguin's unequivocal indenture to the indefatigable processes of empire
that pursue their racist and sexist ends without opposition—or need of adaptation—
around the globe. Pollock, *Avant-Garde Gambits*, 72.

the primitivist enterprise despite its representational complicity with colonial expropriation. I wish to consider two analyses that, doubling and departing from each other as they do, share and rehearse the lesson of colonial and sexual ambivalence: in the encounter with otherness, nobody goes unscathed. As suggestive as both readings are, they do not fully acknowledge that if Gauguin's house of pleasure stands on shaky ground, it is precisely to the degree that its primitivist foundations rely on the example of Polynesian gender dissonance as it manifests sexual possibilities barred European representation. Far from being the result or even the fantasy of imperial omnipotence, Gauguin's paintings comprise a hybridized form of sexual representation that could emerge only in the specific cultural context of the colonial Pacific.

"Noa Noa"

In writing of Gauguin's Tahitian paintings many critics refer to "Noa Noa," the highly artificial journal that represents the time of Gauguin's first stay in Tahiti. Composed on his return to Paris in 1893, "Noa Noa" remains less than pleasing as a literary artifact, although the facsimile edition of the Louvre manuscript version that Gauguin produced in collaboration with the poet Charles Morice has an undeniable visual luminescence. Its watercolors and woodcuts are dispersed enigmatically through the text, and their appeal far outweighs that of the narrative they interrupt and often supersede. And yet it is the narrative not the illustrations of "Noa Noa" to which recent criticism frequently returns, in particular to the woodcutting episode that comprises the fourth chapter. At the end of that chapter's first paragraph are placed a watercolor and woodcut that depict, in the upper hemisphere, a couple in sexual congress—a male and a female figure balled together, belly to belly, with only elbows, knees, and feet breaking the perimeter of the two-toned embrace—and in the lower, a women curled fetally on her side (figure 6).[11] Nicholas Wadley points

---

[11] Figure 6 is a reproduction of page 75 from the so-called Louvre manuscript version. Nicholas Wadley describes the Louvre manuscript as "an enlarged version of the original text as redrafted by Gauguin's collaborator, the poet Charles Morice," and notes that Gauguin's illustrations were for the most part produced in Paris. *Noa Noa:*

6 Paul Gauguin, folio 75 of "Noa Noa" (1896–1903), watercolor and woodcut. Musée du Louvre, Paris. Reproduced with permission from Réunion des Musées Nationaux. Photo RMN.

out that the "upper image of the lovemaking couple" is remarkable "because figures in Gauguin's paintings seldom touch each other, let alone embrace." The sexually explicit image is all the more remarkable, however, because neither it nor the nude beneath it graphically anticipates that the woodcutting episode will comprise an erotic rite of passage occurring between men.[12]

The journal chapter begins with Gauguin's claim that life in Tahiti "every day gets better" as "civilisation leaves [him] bit by bit." The physical transformation he undergoes ("my naked feet, from daily contact with the rock, have got used to the ground, my body, almost always naked, no longer fears the sun") is paralleled by a moral metamorphosis whereby he abandons the competitive and acrimonious forms of European sociability to "function in an animal way, freely," among his Tahitian neighbors, who regard him "as almost one of themselves." A young man, his "natural friend," visits him daily to watch him work and talk with him. "Sometimes in the evening, when I was resting from my day's work," recalls Gauguin, "he would ask me the questions of a young savage who wants to know a lot of things about love in Europe, questions which often embarrassed me."[13]

The chapter then goes on to relate an expedition the artist and the "faultlessly handsome" boy undertake to fell a rosewood tree from which to make a carving. Gauguin follows his young male guide as they climb single file through the dense vegetation of the Tahitian interior. Gauguin recalls that both are naked "except for the loincloth," and "two we certainly were, two friends, he a quite young man and I almost an old man in body and soul, in civilised vices: in lost illusions. His lithe animal body had graceful contours, he walked in front of me sexless. . . ."[14] Gauguin's marginal notes at this moment underscore what he calls "the androgynous aspect of the savage," which he asso-

---

Gauguin's Tahiti, ed. Nicholas Wadley, trans. Jonathan Griffin (Oxford: Phaidon, 1985), 7. Brettell likewise suggests the importance of Paris in engendering Gauguin's interest in illustrated texts (his model was Eugène Delacroix's North African journal) and disputes the routine dating of the production of other of his manuscripts to his Tahitian period. Brettell, "Return to France," 297–98.

[12] *Noa Noa*, ed. Wadley, 145. Wadley nonetheless manages to link both images to their narrative framing so that the difference between the episode's suggestion of homosexual possibility and its illustration of heterosexual intercourse is taken to be no difference at all.

[13] *Noa Noa*, ed. Wadley, 24–25.

[14] *Noa Noa*, ed. Wadley, 25, ellipsis in original.

ciates with the "desire to be for a moment weak, a woman."[15] Trailing after this nonspecific sexual figure, Gauguin becomes disoriented with desire and is visited by a "presentiment of crime, the desire for the unknown, the awakening of evil—Then weariness of the male role, having always to be strong, protective; shoulders that are a heavy load. To be for a moment the weak being who loves and obeys."[16] At this point, "without fear of laws," he approaches the figure before him, but his arousal dissipates as soon as its object presents frontally: "My companion turned at that moment, so that his chest was towards me. The hermaphrodite had vanished; it was a young man, after all; his innocent eyes resembled the limpidity of the water. Calm suddenly came back into my soul." The woodland scene ends not with seduction or rape but the violence of self-discipline as Gauguin expends himself attacking the sought-after tree, "hack[ing] away with the pleasure of sating one's brutality and of destroying something" until his soft hands are bloodied and raw. The renunciation is complete when, pacing behind that naked back on the return journey, Gauguin can "again admire, in front of me, the graceful curves of my young friend—and calmly: curves robust like the tree we were carrying."[17]

Considering this chapter, Peter Brooks remarks that the recollection of the expedition is noteworthy "perhaps especially for the ambivalences of passivity and aggressivity it displays and the confused conception of the homoerotic temptation as alternately domination and submission." From this Brooks concludes that insofar as androgyny "appears to liberate him from European categories of difference," Gauguin is attracted to it. "Yet," he also notes, "that attraction leads [Gauguin] to an interior experience of his own body as bisexual, to a homoerotic temptation that places him in the role of woman and thus must be repudiated. There is a slide away from androgyny which resolves itself in a feeling of guilt dispersed and innocence achieved."[18] In Brooks's account the civilized man, in turning his desire toward a native object, locates in that object an ambivalence that can be taken in, and mastered by, himself, albeit violently. This peculiar relay of identification and desire seems all too familiar, another of those decadent loops through the exotic that replenishes the metropolitan sub-

<hr>

[15] *Noa Noa*, ed. Wadley, 74 n. 42.

[16] *Noa Noa*, ed. Wadley, 25.

[17] *Noa Noa*, ed. Wadley, 28.

[18] Peter Brooks, "Gauguin's Tahitian Body," *Yale Journal of Criticism* 3, no. 2 (1990): 67.

ject via the diminishment of a racially or sexually marked other. Of this sexual detour, Brooks writes:

> The incident might have given Gauguin an occasion to cast doubt on his unproblematic opposition of civilization and the primitive and to reflect on his need for a tropology of Tahitian bodies in order to rework critically a European tradition. But he doesn't in *Noa Noa* achieve this kind of self-reflexiveness, resolving the incident instead in a moment of male bonding with his Tahitian friend and the claim that he has recovered radical innocence. Gauguin is interested in a polymorphous bodiliness, but when it comes to foregrounding, touching, and representing a body, it must be clearly gendered as female, albeit a female body that breaks from the traditional Western sense of female gracefulness, that is more powerful and compact, less distinct from the male. . . . The passage from *Noa Noa* becomes virtually an allegory of a large cultural need to center discourse of the body exclusively on the female body, as if the male body and the temptation of androgyny were too dangerous to handle.[19]

Although Brooks argues insightfully that Gauguin's interest in framing the polymorphous body necessarily confines itself to female subjects, he has nothing more to say about this. Instead of critically interrogating this overdetermined maneuver, Brooks gives himself over to it instead: "This cultural movement may in some sense justify the slippage in my own discussion of the Tahitian body toward exclusively female objects."[20] By declining the dubious invitation the male body extends and restricting his focus to the representation of Polynesian women, Brooks suggests the contractual terms of his sexual identification with Gauguin. In both the passage from "Noa Noa" and the commentary on it, the Tahitian male body, as an object available to a pleasured look, shimmers briefly on the visual (and sexual) horizon, only to fade from view.

Blind

If we consider what is here too blinding to look upon, we discover another way in which Brooks's passage might be said to repeat Gauguin's "slippage." Both text and commentary seem to be teasingly

---

[19] Brooks, "Gauguin's Tahitian Body," 67.
[20] Brooks, "Gauguin's Tahitian Body," 67.

structured around "homoerotic temptation." Brooks's entire discussion of this passage is caged in negatives and casual qualifiers; it appears as the discussion he will not provide. "One could no doubt analyze this passage at some length," he writes, as if that would be a somehow tedious or predictable interpretative byway down which to travel.[21] Strangely, his testimony that the male body as trope is culturally too hot to handle is belied by the analysis he does engage in. Indeed, Brooks is rather eloquent, almost loquacious, about the male body and its engendering of sexual ambivalence and disavowal. He pretends not to know, or not to be interested in, a subject about which he has quite a lot to say all the same. Why the critical ruse? "Homoerotic temptation" functions in both "Noa Noa" and commentary as a kind of erotic or critical lever, but where in Gauguin it triggered a well-rehearsed errancy, a tired shuffle toward and swerve away from the perverse, in Brooks's writing it is under a different sort of pressure. Brooks refuses to substitute "homosexual" for "homoerotic," ringing in an "interior" bisexuality before arriving at the palliative "temptation of androgyny," but he neglects to say anything about that refusal. Written one hundred years apart, text and commentary seem to share the same open secret: it goes without saying that homosexuality is the repudiated act in "Noa Noa" and the repudiated term in Brooks's analysis.

Brooks is content to follow Gauguin's lead and maintain androgyny as the trope through which this arousal must be thought. In both accounts androgyny is the rhetorical figure for a binary heterosexual logic that contains the threat of a homoeroticism that takes the male body as its subject and object, by insisting that one of those bodies be marked effeminately. In this context it is worth recalling that Gauguin, after all, is in no doubt as to the sex of the native figure he follows through the fragrant jungle, nor are we as readers. Furthermore, if, as he pants up that lurid hillside, he is subject to a sexual swoon, the poles he sways between are not male and female but domination and submission—which is what Brooks began by saying but never returned to. Initially subtle, Brooks's analysis finally refuses to follow what we might call the "sodomitical" figurings in Gauguin's writing, as they suggest the troublesome penetrability of bodies, male as well as female. This adjectival usage of *sodomitical* follows that of Lee

---

[21] Brooks, "Gauguin's Tahitian Body," 67.

Edelman, who analyzes "the disturbance of positionality" generated around male-male sexual scenes.[22] The panicky confusion that Edelman argues assails the witness to such scenes proceeds not only from the literal positions taken up by sodomites but more fundamentally from the fact that these poses are figural condensations of a whole raft of consequently disordered relations between front and back, before and after, male and female, homosexual and heterosexual.[23] In "Noa Noa"'s woodcutting episode the sexual desirability of the young man viewed from behind constitutes a perverse spectacle against which the figure of androgyny is rhetorically deployed in order to reassert the proper hierarchical relations between these terms. When the androgynous figure finally presents frontally—"a young man, after all"—any obscure pull toward perversity is effaced by the transparent propriety of "his innocent eyes."

In *Manao tupapau*, a painting from late 1892, a similar logic is at work. The abandonment of frontality once again implicates the viewer in the posture of perversion, but now the primitivist invitation to sodomy can be safely extended across the availability of women, thus guarding or preserving the imagined impenetrability of the male. In both instances, gender difference reconfigures homosexual possibility within a heterosexual paradigm.

Behindsight

Perhaps, then, we should return to the passage from "Noa Noa" and take the time to state the obvious: the thing that sets in train this display of sexual ambivalence is the mere apprehension of a figure viewed—as Freud might say—*a tergo*, from behind. In his more general discussion of primitivist aesthetics, Hal Foster suggests that such

---

[22] Lee Edelman, *Homographesis: Essays in Gay Literary and Cultural Theory* (New York: Routledge, 1994), 183.

[23] In Edelman's account the scandalous possibility of the (male) anus as a site of sexual pleasure disrupts the psychoanalytic narrative that secures heterosexuality through a positing of masculinity and femininity in relation to a phallic economy. What is legible in the sodomitical scene is "its repudiation of the binary logic implicit in male heterosexualisation" and "its all too *visible* dismissal of the threat [of castration] on which the terroristic empire of male heterosexuality has so effectively been erected." Edelman, *Homographesis*, 185, emphasis in original.

"primal" scenes, and the anality they represent, comprise the sexual genesis of primitivism. Citing Freud's "association of tribal peoples with *pregenital* orders of the drives, especially oral and anal stages, an association in which genitality is often correlated with civilisation as achievements beyond 'the primitive,'" Foster draws our attention to the way primitivism and psychoanalysis, emerging in the same historical moment, share certain narratives of cultural and sexual arrest: they both figure the tribal, the feminine, the homosexual as caught in early phases of psychic development.[24] Primitivism then privileges these sites as kinds of regressive destinations, which, once visited, can evidence the shucking off of the repressions of civilization.

Foster argues that the primitivist psychic agenda is not pursued without trauma. Aware of the racism underwriting these modernist discourses, he proposes we "hold to [Freud's] conception of stages but not to its association with tribal peoples. Or, rather, I will reverse the flow of this association: for example, to see anality not as the property of 'the primitive' but as the projection of a particular modern subjectivity onto 'the primitive.' The question then becomes not what is 'primitive anality' but why is it projected as such—out of what desires and fears?"[25] The woodcutting episode related by Gauguin in "Noa Noa" provides Foster the prototype for the primitivist projection of anality onto the racially marked other. Foster argues that the "ambivalence" foregrounded in the Tahitian encounter is related to the doubled fantasmatics of anality whereby the traumatic recognition that sexual difference is founded through castration is disavowed by a dual identification with agents of penetration and receptivity. Freud's Wolf Man provides the model of a "primitive" subject who "when faced with a castrative threat or a genital crisis" regresses "to a pregenital order, in which the subject oscillates between an anal *eroticism*, a passive masochistic mode (associated, as usual in Freud, with the feminine and the homosexual), and its active complement, an anal *sadism*—an oscillation expressive of a great ambivalence of psychosexual position."[26]

Thus for Foster the primitivist project works a kind of imperialist renewal and at the same time bears witness to the "crisis of white het-

---

[24] Hal Foster, "'Primitive' Scenes," *Critical Inquiry* 20 (1993): 71–72, emphasis in original.

[25] Foster, "'Primitive' Scenes," 72.

[26] Foster, "'Primitive' Scenes," 78.

erosexual masculinity" at the core of the primitivist encounter.[27] Consequently, in his unraveling of the skeins of identification and desire that tangle across scenes such as the woodcutting episode, he repeatedly reminds us not to "mistake a desire for mastery for the real thing."[28] Foster insists that the historical prevalence of images in which "racial others, male and female, are presented as passive" subjects available to a "colonialist gaze [that] seems to double a sexual gaze in a vision of masculinist mastery" is an indication that exactly such a representation is required to forestall the recognition of its psychic unsustainability. "Again and again," artists such as Gauguin

> map racial onto sexual difference and vice versa in a conundrum of oppositions of black and white, female and male, nature and culture, passive and active, homosexual and heterosexual. However, since ambivalence governs these mappings—since "the primitive" both attracts and repels these artists, since they both desire and identify with it— such oppositions are pressured to the point where they begin to falter, where the white heterosexual masculinity founded on them begins to crack.[29]

But just as these fissures in the psychic foundations of "white heterosexual masculinity" appear, Foster stresses the soundness of their historical support: "However," he writes, "to underscore the fragility of primitivist mastery, its basis in desire and fantasy, is not to diminish its actuality, the reality of power relations and domination effects in the imperialist encounter."[30]

Where for Solomon-Godeau the historical reality of imperialism is continuous with the psychic paradigm of masculine primitivism, for Foster the two are discontinuous although they stand in equally motivated relation. Foster's approach, with its historically correct emphasis on psychoanalysis as one of the foundational discourses of modernism, runs the danger of cutting the aesthetic object off from the context of its colonial production, although that very decision simultaneously enables the political invocation of an "imperialist encounter" the "reality" of which is already known and beyond dispute.

[27] Foster, "'Primitive' Scenes," 102.
[28] Foster, "'Primitive' Scenes," 80.
[29] Foster, "'Primitive' Scenes," 81.
[30] Foster, "'Primitive' Scenes," 75–76.

Both imperialism and primitivism become in this account pan-discourses that sweep any number of actors and histories into their uniform collectivity.

Against this impulse, Stephen Eisenman insists that Gauguin's Pacific work be read as a situated discourse that is everywhere inscribed with specific marks of racial and sexual difference that index the Polynesian context in which they arose. For Eisenman, Gauguin's Pacific paintings are the "incipient" site for a "critical primitivism" that registers both the sexual and racial ideologies of colonialism and the counterdiscourse of indigenous resistance to European modernity.[31] This critical quality can be demonstrated if Gauguin's paintings are rethought formally. They can be seen to engage a hybridized aesthetic that is neither conservative nor progressive per se but a sign that Western hegemonies were compromised before the complexity of Polynesian cultures and traditions. The formal and thematic experiments of *Manao tupapau*, Gauguin's Tahitian rephrasing of Manet's *Olympia*, arise at the intersection of two distinctive sexual regimes that differently cast sexual possibilities across and within gender. In this painting the female figure signifies a sexual availability that is more properly that of the *māhū*, a male-sexed but gender-liminal figure familiar within Tahitian society. The incorporation of this figure and the sexual possibilities it represents into the tradition of the European nude is not in itself radically transformative. Rather, the effect of that inclusion is to make the painting the site of a complex readjustment of relations of power that are newly overlayed and distributed across racially marked and gendered bodies.

Copy

In the year of his departure to the South Seas, Gauguin spent eight days before Manet's *Olympia* in the Musée du Luxembourg producing a copy that would eventually find its way into Degas's private collection. The scandal that erupted at the first public showing of *Olympia* is well known to anyone who has read T. J. Clark's *Painting of Mod-*

---

[31] Eisenman, *Gauguin's Skirt*, 201. Nicholas Thomas makes a similar point about colonial art more generally in his introduction to *Double Vision: Art Histories and Colonial Histories in the Pacific*, ed. Nicholas Thomas and Diane Losche (Cambridge: Cambridge University Press, 1999), 2–3.

ern Life. Clark's thesis about the contradictory nature of capitalism's investment in female sexuality and the slippery aesthetics such contradiction implies leans heavily on his discussion of Manet's "disarticulated" rendering of the model's body in *Olympia.* If, as Clark argues, the sexualized modernity of the model is conveyed in the way the formal curves of the reclining figure are contorted—"its knees dislocated and arms broken" so that "Olympia's whole body is matter of smooth hard edges and deliberate intersections" caught in abrupt shifts from light to dark—and the way the sharp line of the shoulders and the far nipple breaking the bounding line of that arm are both incommensurate with the lack of definition of the model's right breast, then this would come as no surprise to Gauguin, whose copy exaggerates precisely these features.[32] When combined with the idiosyncratic facial features of the model, these compositional effects, Clark contends, attribute to her a modern subjectivity unlike the embodied vacancy of the traditional nude, a subjectivity that is further pressed on the viewer by the formulaic handling of the black female servant. The self-evident femininity of the nude "upon which the spectator is free to impose his imaginary definitions" has been formally compromised, dismantled and replaced by a cold circuit of signs that no longer reify the female body but foreground its materiality. Manet's aesthetic, Clark argues, emerges as modernity writes itself across the sexual body.[33] When the social relations of mass culture mark women with the signature of class, Olympia is, and is seen to be, a working girl: she is prostitute, not courtesan.

When the look of the viewer meets this recalcitrant female object, one capable of a stare saturated with its own desires and demands, the terms of consensuality that the nude mystifies become open to cynical wrangling: "Olympia . . . looks out at the viewer in a way which obliges him to imagine a whole fabric of sociality in which this look might make sense and include him—a fabric of offers, places, payments, particular powers, and status which is still open to negotiation."[34] This look, marked as sexually solicitous, explains the incoherence of the viewing position that the work, historically, implies. Once the viewer's look is returned in this way, the scopic field of the

---

[32] T. J. Clark, *The Painting of Modern Life: Paris in the Art of Manet and His Followers* (Princeton: Princeton University Press, 1984), 134.

[33] Clark, *Painting of Modern Life,* 135.

[34] Clark, *Painting of Modern Life,* 133.

painting is defined as that charged zone across which gazes may lock and challenge the immunity of vision. The imaginary plenitude of the nude has been eclipsed by an insufficiency that touches both object and viewer; the sovereignty of sight is no longer unassailable. The critical hysteria that greeted the unveiling of *Olympia* is symptom of this incoherence—the ways of seeing that Olympia assigns her audience are deeply fraught: to the Parisian public she is cadaver, insult, whore.[35]

Clark's analysis traces the enunciative address of Manet's painting as it functions in its historical moment. Although the outrage assigned *Olympia*'s contemporaneous viewer is no longer assigned us, signs of that incoherence remain coded in the formal innovations and radical iconographics of the work. In this respect Gauguin is an exact interpreter of Manet: *Manao tupapau* similarly stigmatizes the position of the viewing subject, but now the formal incoherence of the painting is played out in a specifically primitivist (and colonialist) register that is supercharged by knowledge of Polynesian same-sex sexual possibility, particularly as it manifests in the gender liminality of the Tahitian *māhū*.

Roll

Gauguin took with him to Tahiti a photographic reproduction of *Olympia* and had it to hand in 1892 as he produced *Manao tupapau* (figure 7).[36] Where Gauguin's presentation of the reclining female most obviously departs from Manet's is that the Tahitian model, Teha'amana, is splayed belly down and faces the other way with her head to the right of the frame. It is as though the Parisian original has been brazenly rotated and turned onto her flip side. Yet this obvious difference shouldn't obscure the fact that much else in the formal disposition of the female figure is a citation of the Manet. We might think

[35] For Clark on the contemporary response to *Olympia*, see *Painting of Modern Life*, 79–89.

[36] Early in "Noa Noa" Gauguin relates an incident in which an unnamed native woman browses through the eclectic collection of paintings and photographs that cluttered his Tahitian studio until her attention is caught by a reproduction of Manet's *Olympia*, which she takes for a depiction of the artist's wife. *Noa Noa*, ed. Wadley, 21.

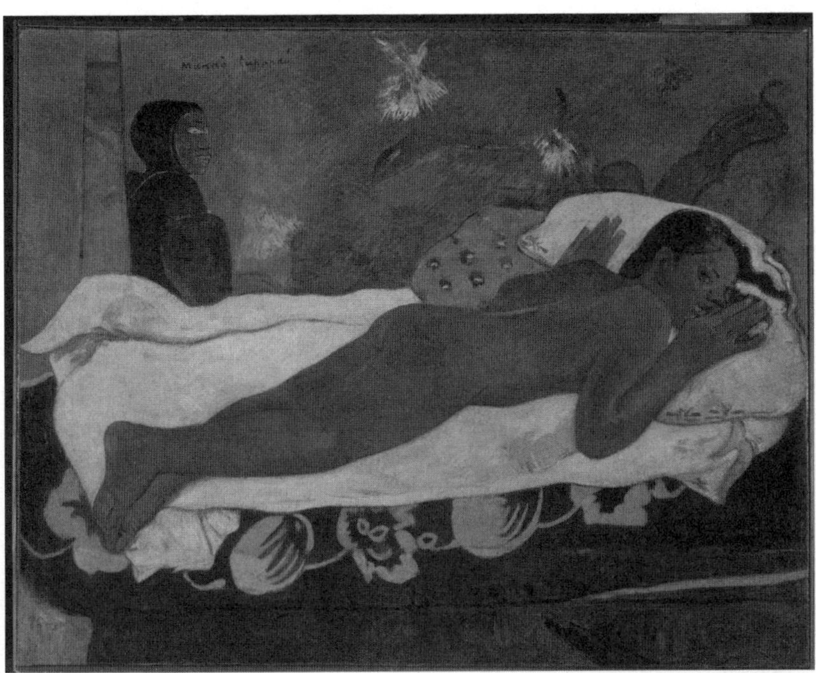

7 Paul Gauguin, *Spirit of the Dead Watching* (*Manao tupapau*) (1892), oil on burlap
mounted on canvas, 28½ x 36⅜″. Albright-Knox Art Gallery, Buffalo, New York,
A. Conger Goodyear Collection, 1965. Reproduced with permission.

of those hands as deriving directly from the 1865 canvas, but more
than that we recognize the way the curves of the body are deliberately
broken—legs cross, elbows bend. The body's outlines against the pale
sheet are also the same, heavily scored, where those of the face are
slub. Similarly, the fall of the back seems vaguely defined—the spine
and left shoulder blade won't compose readily, and the play of light on
the cleft of the buttocks and the right hip and shoulder seem to throw
the small of the back out as though the torso were awkwardly twisted.
Then there is the way the body tilts or slides off the plane of the bed
into a different vertical, as though there is a slightly skewed perspective at work here that is capable of altering the spatial depth of the
painting. The strict formal citation of Manet thus also draws attention to the precarious rear attitude of the Polynesian model, reinforcing the racial innovation of Gauguin's canvas as a matter of positioning.

Gauguin's account of the inception of this painting has—as he intended—been overly useful in unraveling its Polynesian symbolics, but his comments might rather be read as giving clues to a European imaginary. In a letter to his Danish wife, Mette, in which he instructs her in the promotion of his Tahitian work, Gauguin insists that the pose of the woman on the bed is of primary interest: "In that position a mere hint and it is indecent. Yet that is the way I want it. . . . A girl from our own part of the world would be afraid of being caught in that position (women here not at all)."[37] And again, in the notebook he dedicated to his daughter Aline, he returns to the indecency of the painting and locates it in the face-down posture:

> In this rather daring position, quite naked on a bed, what might a young Kanaka girl be doing? Preparing for love? This is indeed in her character, but it is indecent and I do not want that. Sleeping, after the act of love? But that is still indecent. The only possible thing is fear. What kind of fear? Certainly not the fear of Susannah surprised by the Elders. That does not happen in Oceania. The *tupapau* [spirit of the dead] is just the thing. . . . According to Tahitian beliefs, the title *Manao tupapau* has a double meaning . . . either she thinks of the ghost or the ghost thinks of her.[38]

Gaugin adds, "This [aforementioned] genesis is written for those who always have to know the whys and wherefores. Otherwise the picture is simply a study of a Polynesian nude."[39] In both accounts the carefully laid signifier of indigenous meaning, the totemic head occupying the place vacated by Manet's black servant, is a blind, a symbolic device leading away from where Gauguin locates the perversity of this painting—in the stance of the girl. It is as though the scandal of the pose for the European requires a cultural alibi, hence the iconographic resort to native superstition.[40] Obviously, then, we need to refuse the

---

[37] Letter from Paul Gauguin to his wife, Mette (née Gad), Copenhagen, 8 December 1892, in *Paul Gauguin: The Writings of a Savage*, ed. Daniel Guérin, trans. Eleanor Levieux (New York: Viking Press, 1978), 63–64.

[38] Passage from Paul Gauguin, *Cahier pour Aline*, 1893, quoted in Claire Frèches-Thory, catalog note 154, "Manao tupapau," in *Art of Paul Gauguin*, ed. Brettell et al., 281.

[39] Quoted in Frèches-Thory, "Manao tupapau," 281.

[40] Pollock is also interested in the model's posture, which she reads as discomfiting the artist, but scarcely before she is able to credit that anxiety to Gauguin, she

lure of that false lead and wrench discussion of *Manao tupapau* away from speculation about the nocturnal imaginings of the native girl toward those of her viewer.

Rear Vision

If we consider both the position of the girl on the bed and the positionality of the implied viewer, then we can say that *Manao tupapau* configures a peculiar erotics: an erotics from the back, not of the back. The figure on the bed—like the young man moving through the jungle in "Noa Noa"—is viewed by someone standing behind her. This perspective becomes clearer if we consider the different vantage provided by a later reworking of the same pose in a small pastel Gauguin produced in Paris in 1895 of his Javanese mistress, Annah (figure 8). Here the viewer is situated on the same parallel as the head and shoulders of the sleeping model; our glance moves across the slant of the body until the faded dissolve of the feet returns us to the calm locus of the head. The viewer is unimplicated in this scene; the self-containment of the sleeper is inviolate, our looking as free from reproach as the figure herself. Furthermore, the way the sway of the back accents the wasp waist of the female model, which is then rounded out by the soft belly underside and the depth of the buttocks, is in contrast to the stolidity, the chunky heft, of the Tahitian figure in *Manao tupapau*, whose gender is less distinctly marked.[41]

The viewer of the bedded figure in *Manao tupapau* is situated otherwise than the viewer of Annah. The figure in the smaller pastel lies

---

comes to inhabit it herself. For Pollock, the prospect of *a tergo* sex becomes the very index of a masculinist European depravity that brooks no possibility of a Tahitian feminine subjectivity. If in her argument the scandal of the painting initially resides with Gauguin, it quickly makes an odd shift to the scandal of *a tergo* sex itself. See Pollock, *Avant-Garde Gambits*, 70–71.

[41] In *Art of Paul Gauguin* Brettell finds gender differently distributed across these two works. Comparing the pastel with *Manao tupapau*, he considers the thinner figure of Annah to be more "androgynous," stating that "without the wisp of hair, the nearly invisible earring, and the gentle swelling of the chest, one could almost imagine that the model was male. Even [Teha'amana], who could scarcely be called archetypically feminine, projects her sexual identity more strongly in the painting *Manao tupapau*." Richard Brettell, catalog note 161, "Reclining Nude," in *Art of Paul Gauguin*, ed. Brettell et al., 309.

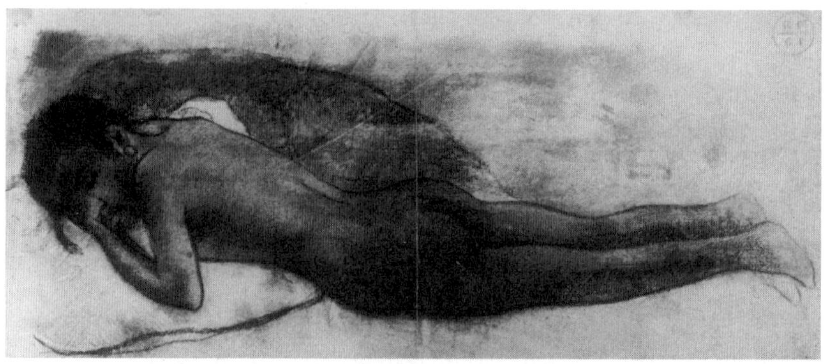

8 Paul Gauguin, *Reclining Nude* (c. 1894–95), charcoal, black chalk, and pastel on paper. From the collection of Mrs. Robert B. Eicholz (U.S.A.). Reproduced with permission from the Witt Library, Courtauld Institute of Art, London.

stable on a near horizontal, but the solid angled legs of the reclining Teha'amana accentuate a diagonal rise that the viewer's look must follow, encroaching upward along the prone body toward that strangely obscured face and irresolute stare. Thus the watcher is positioned at the foot of the bed, which is precisely aligned with the watcher in painted space—the specter of the dead. Once this connection has been made, once we recognize that our viewpoint aligns with the totemic head's, it is as though the scene is also transected on another axis across the foot of the bed. The drawing of this imaginary line further swivels the girl on the bed; it presents her more from behind than from the side, exaggerating the awkwardness of that pose. Nancy Mowell Matthews comments, as well, on the "slightly raised" buttocks "turned toward" the viewer and on the "visible curved stroke of orange paint [that] calls attention to the point of entry between them."[42] Everything conspires to present the subject *a tergo,* or from behind. It is as though none of the coordinates in the picture plane is reliable, and in Brooks's phrase, the girl on the bed starts "slipping forward toward the frontal plane of the canvas in a way that challenges the tra-

[42] Nancy Mowell Matthews, *Paul Gauguin: An Erotic Life* (New Haven: Yale University Press, 2001), 183.

ditional space—and posture of dominance—of the spectator," as she has been threatening to do all along.[43]

The sexual immunity under which the classical nude is viewed is compromised by this rear presentation, which is spatially devised for maximum exposure. The invulnerability of the viewing position is further weakened once that alignment between the position of the watcher and that of the death totem has been drawn. Floating in the confusing depths of the virtual background but also level on the flat of the picture plane, the profiled head of the specter presents a frontal eye that watches over the viewer as much as, the French title tells us, the specter watches over her, the native girl. The viewer has become locked before an alienating mirror. Any visual access granted over the girl on the bed is crossed by that weird gaze, which places the viewer under an unflinching surveillance, formally arrested inside the perverse dynamics of the painting's field.

Hesitation

The formal innovations of *Manao tupapau*, particularly its experiments with color and spatial depth, are such that the indigenous superstition Gauguin cynically coded into the painting seems to reach outside the frame and contaminate the colonial viewing position, disputing its sexual impunity. In Foster's terms this might be thought an uncanny return, except that Gauguin has deliberately plotted this ambivalent effect. In another passage from the Louvre manuscript, he recalls the origin of this particular painting:

> It was one in the morning when I got home. Having at that moment very little oil in the house—my stock was due to be replenished—the lamp had gone out, and the room was in darkness when I went in. I felt afraid and, more still, mistrustful. Surely the bird has flown. I struck matches. . . . Motionless, naked, lying face down on the bed, her eyes immeasurably larger from fear, [Teha'amana] looked at me and seemed not to know me. I too was caught for several moments by a strange feeling of uncertainty. [Teha'amana]'s terror was contagious. I had the illu-

---

[43] Brooks, "Gauguin's Tahitian Body," 70.

sion that a phosphorescent light was streaming from her staring eyes. Never had I seen her so beautiful, so frighteningly beautiful.[44]

In narrativizing the undoing of the male voyeur in the cross-cultural contact zone, in entrapping him in a scene of primitivist perversion, Gauguin sketches a rudimentary theory of colonial contagion. The certainty of Western enlightenment (the oil in the lamp) is extinguished in the native locale, washed over by other ghostly illuminations, and it is this contaminatory logic that the painting formally inscribes. Gauguin's painting records what Foster would call "primitivist ambivalence" with all the efficiency of a stereoscope—it is technically able to present two images as one. Conflating the native and the sodomitically perverse, *Manao tupapau* stages an interference between European regression and indigenous truth in an inescapably formalist register. Gauguin's decorative experiments with the flat of the picture plane keep flicking us between primitivist alternatives—perversion and *tapu*, say—in a kind of optical switchback.[45] Therein, perhaps, lies the attraction and menace of this painting. If in its representation of a primitivist scopic field, it revises the space of observation and structures a gaze that invades the seamlessness of looking, if it unsettles vision—and hermeneutics—with hesitations and anxieties, with ambivalent doublings, it also suggests the impossibility of ever falling outside that scene. Insofar as *Manao tupapau* deploys the blank enunciative address of modernism, it installs the position of the viewing subject as permanently recruitable to a primitivist thematics. It can replay again and again the ambivalent falterings of colonial discourse within the privileged—allegedly ahistoric—space of the artwork.

Brooks, however, attaches a very different interpretation to Gauguin's representation of the reclining figure in *Manao tupapau* and suggests that the precariously rear presentation of the woman erases the conventional dominance of the viewer in relation to the female subject by implicating him in an economy of sexual gift that remains definitive of Pacific encounter:

<hr>

[44] *Noa Noa*, ed. Wadley, 38 and 78 n. 61.

[45] *Tapu* is the correct name for the systems of restrictive ban that fall across Tahitian bodies and their social practices. However, what Gauguin seems to be installing in his painting more accurately recalls the notion of an evil eye, which in the Western tradition has always been the figure that oversees borders and the placement of the thresholds of sexuality and mortality.

Like the body of *Olympia*, that in *Manao tupapau* is offered to the spectator's gaze, though not frontally this time, rather in a pose that refuses to be a pose, refuses the sense of self-display that one finds in *Olympia* and the distinct impression given by Manet's girl that she is available, for a price. Gauguin's nude is also available, but in a more unselfconscious way and without connotations of venality. As an Olympia turned over, the nude of *Manao tupapau* may suggest a comment on the problematics of penetrability and impenetrability posed by Gauguin—may suggest, to use his term, a greater "animality" than that evoked by the classic poses of the nude.

The body of *Manao tupapau* . . . is offered to our gaze in such a way that its nakedness, conceived as natural to the woman herself, is made a natural, right object of vision, without overtones of sin or commerce. . . . In contrast to the attributes of *Olympia* that betoken the women's exchange value . . . those of *Manao tupapau* suggest an economy of the gift, as it would be defined by Marcel Mauss: the free and generous offering which must be responded to by a corresponding gift—which may here be the painting itself. And the gift of the *potlatch*, as Georges Bataille points out, is related to the creation of sacred objects: objects that have no use value, that belong, not to an economy of exchange and accumulation, but to an economy of waste, glorious expenditure. Gauguin, one might say, is attempting to reach back beyond the economy of exchange to that of the gift—as it were, denying Wallis's version of Tahiti in order to resurrect Bougainville's vision.[46]

Brooks appears to endorse Gauguin's primitivist project but only as it avails itself of the mechanism of the female body. The relation between the exaggeration of the *a tergo* posture and an economy of waste allows "animality" to stand in this reading where "anality" does in Foster's.[47] In Brooks's interpretation the sodomitical invitation that was refused in the scene from "Noa Noa" is restated in *Manao tupapau*, only now the rear penetrability of the native figure is extravagantly indulged, leaving as it does the "sacred" impenetrability of the male intact. Sodomitical imaginings are thus rendered safe as they play across the several availabilities, genital and anal, of the female body.[48]

---

[46] Brooks, "Gauguin's Tahitian Body," 70–71.

[47] The Freudian connotations of "gift" and its association via waste with anality can surely not be lost on Brooks.

[48] Foster reads the *Manao tupapau* pose as "bestial," as representing an anal sadism

9 Paul Gauguin, *Self-Portrait with Hat* (1893–94), oil. Musée d'Orsay, Paris. Reproduced with permission from Réunion des Musées Nationaux. Photo RMN, Franck Raux.

10 Paul Gauguin, *Portrait of William Molard* (verso of *Self-Portrait with Hat*) (1893–94), oil. Musée d'Orsay, Paris. Reproduced with permission from Réunion des Musées Nationaux. Photo RMN.

And yet, as Eisenman has argued, Gauguin throughout his time in the Pacific was repeatedly exposed to male bodies offering themselves to effeminate pleasures in the example of the gender-liminal *māhū*. Eisenman suggests that Gauguin consciously identified with the sexual status of the *māhū*, going so far as to cultivate the ambiguous appearance of a *taata vahine* ("man-woman") through the adoption of native dress.[49] But if the representation of the female model Teha'amana likely indexes Gauguin's knowledge of *māhū*, it also reveals that the male–male sexual possibilities suggested by that knowledge are crucially relocated on a body known to be female. *Manao tupapau* both indulges and checks the sodomitical impulse: the open invitation it makes of the face-down female figure preserves the seamless closure considered proper to the male European body even as it signals the pleasure it is clenched against.

This gendered displacement of male–male sexual possibilities known but turned down is further evidenced in Gauguin's later citation of the same painting. Presented here together, the two images that comprise figures 9 and 10 are reverse sides of a single canvas. On the recto appears a self-portrait of Gauguin in which a transposed *Manao tupapau* in a squared yellow frame takes up the high right background. On the verso is a portrait of Gauguin's friend, William Molard, who lived in the apartment above Te Faruru, the artist's studio in the rue Vercingétorix, and with whose teenage stepdaughter, Judith, Gauguin established a sexual liaison even as he lived with his Javanese mistress below. Françoise Cachin tells us that Gauguin "gave Molard this two-sided canvas as a sign of his friendship and gratitude."[50] Perhaps, then, this is the structure of the painting as sexual gift: it figures as part of an affectional exchange between heterosexually identified men that,

---

that is one of the poles to which primitivist ambivalence swings in order to disavow any pull toward that other pole, an anal eroticism assumed in oneself through pleasures considered to be passive or masochistic. Once again, he insists that these expressions of sadistic "masculinist mastery" bespeak their opposite, an anxiety that can never be allayed no matter how aggressive the attempt. See Foster, "'Primitive' Scenes," 79.

[49] See Eisenman, *Gauguin's Skirt*, 21, 27–28, 91–151. For a further discussion of Gauguin's awareness of *māhū* and the explicit heterosexism of Brooks's reading of his work, see Rod Edmond, *Representing the South Pacific: Colonial Discourse from Cook to Gauguin* (Cambridge: Cambridge University Press, 1997), 246–64.

[50] Françoise Cachin, catalog note 164, "Self-Portrait with Hat (recto); Portrait of William Molard (verso)," in *Art of Paul Gauguin*, ed. Brettell et al., 312.

even as it avails itself of tropes of perversion and reversal, must guard against the confusion with homosexuality and thus revives that strained though necessary alibi, the rearwardly prone body of a girl.

Gauguin's response to the male–male sexual possibility represented by Tahitian *māhū* has none of the nonchalance exhibited by Cook's men when they engaged with Hawaiian *aikāne*. At the end of the nineteenth century, European understanding of same-sex sexual capacity hardened into the utterly modern diagnostics of sexual inversion and perversity, whose outcome would be the bifurcated system of homosexual and heterosexual identification that dominates the next one hundred years. The sexual aesthetics of primitivism occur at this juncture, certainly, but they are less a distortion of Pacific sexual history than the logical conclusion of a century and a half of cross-cultural encounter in which European and Polynesian sexual systems continually influence and codetermine each other.

6 *Fa'afafine: Queens of Samoa* and Sexual Elision

Throughout this book I have argued that Pacific texts of encounter register, as if subliminally, the transformation of European understandings of male sexual possibility. The sexual interlocking of European and Polynesian is not confined to the past, however, but continues to engage in the contemporary postcolonial moment. In this final chapter I demonstrate that the question of European-Pacific sexual difference—of whether or not Western and indigenous categories of sexual identity coincide with each other and if so in what ways—continues to be a highly fraught one. The categories of sexual identity available at the end of the twentieth century and beginning of the twenty-first obviously exceed those available to the men who accompanied Cook. That much goes without saying, as does the related point that those earlier men did not yet have the need to define themselves in such sexual terms. However, the modern system of sexual registration whereby Western subjects understand themselves to be defined in relation to a primary distinction between heterosexual and homosexual orientations has taken shape through the encounter with indigenous sexual regimes. It is my argument that just as the spectacle of Polynesian sexual difference has been integral to shaping such a system, a system indentured to a bifurcated understanding of sexuality as either hetero- or homo-, so too is it integral to its transformation.

The subject of this chapter is a recent documentary on Samoan *fa'afafine.* Brightening an otherwise dull Tuesday night's viewing with the promise that it would display Samoan men engaging in conduct said to escape European sexual definitions, *Fa'afafine: Queens of Samoa,* directed by Caroline Harker and bearing the state-funded stamp of New Zealand on Air, was broadcast on New Zealand network television on 29 August 1995. Harker's documentary insists that the gender-liminal *fa'afafine* who are its subject are not to be understood in relation to European categories of identification such as gay, transvestite, or transsexual. I couldn't agree more and I couldn't agree less. *Fa'afafine* are not homosexuals, nor are they transvestites or transsexual subjects, and yet, perversely, my criticism of *Queens of Samoa* is on the grounds of this strenuous agreement. It is the ease with which the documentary discounts the relevance of those other categories that gives me pause: its insistence on definitional difference works to barricade Polynesian and European sexual identities against each other. Where I have been arguing for the mutually transformative effects of historical encounter on the sexualized bodies of all colonial subjects, the documentary sequesters its Samoan subjects apart from *palāgi* culture.[1] In effect, the documentary repeats the diachronic maneuver of discovery, assigning *fa'afafine* to a previous time and space—the "traditional"—which both precedes the moment of observation and continues beyond it. This hard and fast separation into traditional and modern identities is necessarily indifferent to the synchronicity and proximity of those differences. *Fa'afafine* are not gay, transvestites, or transsexual, nor can they occupy the same space— the same place, the same time—as those sexual others. As a chronotope the Pacific has always allowed this kind of differentiation, as if there were two clocks set at the moment of contact, the one counting up the seconds of history, the other holding to the mean time of some imagined past. The traditional can at any moment be invoked against the transactions of history, providing either its justification or its challenge. *Queens of Samoa,* in holding to the idea that *fa'afafine* are a traditional Samoan category, refuses to acknowledge that the difference the category of *fa'afafine* represents must resonate against those other distinctly modern categories of sexual identification—the homosex-

---

[1] *Palāgi* is a Samoan word in relatively common use among both Samoan and white New Zealanders, particularly in social settings in which the two groups have frequent and familiar contact, meaning non-Samoan or European, depending on the context.

ual, the transvestite, the transsexual—to whose historical formation it has itself contributed.

This chapter is an attempt to reframe these issues of sexual difference more productively. A gay reading of the Pacific, such as this book might be said to comprise, must always be wary of indenturing itself to a universal homosexuality that finds everywhere (but most especially in the overtly sexualized Pacific) evidence of its own morphologies. In my critique of the documentary I attempt to read the category of *fa'afafine* not for its absolute difference from homosexuality, transvestiture, or transsexuality but to ask how those categories and that of *fa'afafine* cannot avoid interpellating each other in the contemporary Pacific. This is not to subsume *fa'afafine* within those other categories but to break open their definitional stranglehold and examine the near universal rule that assumes that all desire must be thought in relation to homosexual-heterosexual difference. Gay criticism, particularly that enabled by the work of Eve Kosofsky Sedgwick, even as it has rightly challenged the heterosexist complacency of much thinking about sex and gender, has reified the opposition between heterosexuality and homosexuality into the defining signature of modern conceptualizations of sexuality itself. To reify homosexual difference in this way is to elide other categories of sexual personhood. If I now insist on the salience of the categories of homosexuality, transvestism, and transsexuality to *fa'afafine*, that is also to insist on the salience of *fa'afafine* to those categories, from which it nevertheless remains distinct. This double insistence might force a new understanding of each category, whether Polynesian or European, and suggest finer calibrations of difference than can be accommodated on a sexual grid defined by the strict axes of homosexual-heterosexual distinction.

Caution

Since first contact, Western curiosity has been excited by the intermediate gender categories of the islands of Polynesia. *Fa'afafine*—literally "in the way of a woman"—is the Samoan term for anatomically male individuals who adopt behavioral attributes associated with the female gender. The Tahitian and contemporary Hawaiian equivalent is *māhū;* the Tongan, *fakaleitī*. "In all of these languages," Niko

Besnier explains, "these terms can function as nouns to refer to a person, as verbs to refer to a demeanor or action and often also as adverbs to specify the manner in which an action is being performed."[2] To bluntly translate *fa'afafine, māhū,* or *fakaleitī* as transgenderism sacrifices the syntactic elasticity of the multivocal Polynesian terms and removes the context-specific valences of their usage, which might, for instance, be better preserved in a term like "camp." Questions of translation and of the applicability of Western sexual description to Polynesian behavior are at the heart of both this chapter and the documentary it analyzes.

The signature gesture of the *Queens of Samoa,* the epistemic burden of its broadcast hour, is to insist on the distinction between *fa'afafine* and homosexuality. Whether or not this lesson was learned by its prime-time audience, another should not have been lost on its homosexual viewers, namely, that such gestures of cultural relativism are fully co-optable to a homophobia already proficient in erecting a difference without to forestall a difference within. To make this point is not to deny the specificity of *fa'afafine* and its nonsynonymity with homosexuality but to suggest, as Besnier does, that neither category is as seamless as the documentary assumes and that much is to be gained analytically by maintaining the definitional incoherencies of each. Writing of the relationship between gender liminality and male-to-male sexual acts in Polynesian contexts, Besnier demonstrates that "partaking in homosexual activities is neither a necessary nor a sufficient criterion for gender-liminal status." Contrary to Western conceptualizations of gay identity that place a "defining" emphasis on sexual orientation, in Polynesia "sexual relations with men are seen as an optional *consequence* of gender liminality, rather than its determiner, prerequisite or primary attribute."[3] In Besnier's formulation "optional" refers to an elective relationship between gender-liminal subjects and homosexual activities. However, the emphasis carried by *"consequence"* suggests that gender liminality overdetermines the relation of *fa'afafine* to those activities; that is, it announces the availability of gender-liminal subjects for same-sex sexual acts whether or

[2] Niko Besnier, "Polynesian Gender Liminality through Time and Space," in *Third Sex, Third Gender: Beyond Dimorphism in Culture and History,* ed. Gilbert Herdt (New York: Zone Books, 1994), 286.

[3] Besnier, "Polynesian Gender Liminality," 299, 300.

not they participate in them. Equally, Besnier's formulation extends a discretionary privilege to the nonliminal men who voluntarily engage in sexual acts with *fa'afafine* or *fakaleitī*. So unmarked is the category of the male who has sex with *fa'afafine* that at moments in Besnier's argument, all Samoan and Tongan men except *fa'afafine* and *fakaleitī* themselves are effectively implicated: "While not all gender-liminal individuals have sex with nonliminal men, they are always perceived as a possible sexual conquest by men in societies like Samoa and Tonga."[4] All men are categorically entangled in the sexual possibilities figured forth by *fa'afafine* even as they stand outside gender-liminal behaviors or identifications.

Although neither participant in such sexual acts is to be assumed homosexual, Besnier's more recent work on Tongan *fakaleitī* draws attention to, while deferring investigation of, "gay and lesbian overseas Tongans" whose frequent return to their home islands plays an "important brokering role between gay and lesbian communities in New Zealand, Hawaii, and California and *leitī* in Tonga."[5] Thus Besnier suggests the possibility of overlap between, if not the mutual permeation of, gender liminality and homosexuality. *Queens of Samoa* might be located at precisely this definitional juncture, but rather than address a difference eroded by the migratory transnational profile of contemporary Polynesian culture, the documentary registers the contradictory pressures of its postcolonial moment by demanding that the threatened overlap of *fa'afafine* and homosexuality be forestalled with a typologizing gesture that seeks to secure the boundaries of the first term against the invasiveness of the second.

Voice

Within the limits of its broadcast hour *Queens of Samoa* presents a pointed narrative about colonialism and its corrosive effects on a Samoan culture presumed to be as knowable and uniform prior to contact as it is in its diasporic moment. For all its historical lightness, this

---

[4] Besnier, "Polynesian Gender Liminality," 300.
[5] Niko Besnier, "Sluts and Superwomen: The Politics of Gender Liminality in Urban Tonga," *Ethnos* 62, nos. 1–2 (1997): 11. See also Besnier, "Polynesian Gender Liminality," 304.

editorial account of the contaminatory effect of contact is leadenly advanced at the expense of other specifically sexual narratives or plots, lodged in the particular life histories of the *fa'afafine* informants, which nonetheless make themselves heard against the grain of the documentary. Jay Prosser has recently drawn attention to the way transsexuality, as a self-authored discourse, is always represented as a narrative that involves a spatial or geographic component: "Transition as a geographic trope applies to transsexual narratives; that is, transsexuality as a passage through space, a journey from one location to another. In this sense transition serves as a key means by which transsexuals represent their relations not only to gendered belonging but to sexual communities and politics (lesbian, gay, straight, queer, and, most recently, transgendered)."[6]

Prosser's work is highly suggestive in this context, for the geographic journey undertaken by *fa'afafine*, as it is recorded in the documentary, is a strangely one-way affair. Nearly all the adult *fa'afafine* subjects who appear in the documentary reside in Auckland, suggesting that the actual trajectory of sexual subjecthood involves an almost inevitable transition from island culture to a Pacific metropole heavily marked by the presence and politics of gay and transgendered communities in which cross-racial interactions are more habitual than in the surrounding majoritarian culture. Yet representationally speaking, the documentary insists on a different trajectory, not from Samoa to New Zealand but from New Zealand to Samoa. The journey its subjects are asked to undertake is never a transition into a postcolonial space such as Auckland might represent but always a return, a homeward journey back to a location—inevitably Samoa—assumed to be beyond (and before) such hybridization. In the logic of the documentary the only place *fa'afafine* make sense is in the traditional context of Samoa, but despite this assertion, *Queens of Samoa* also records that the more likely context in which *fa'afafine* must make sense of themselves is contemporary Auckland.

The opening sound and image tracks collude in a frenzy of "Samoanicity" as the documentary cuts rapidly between such iconically weighted images as palm leaves, coconut milk splashing on a rock, and a dancer with traditional headdress, the continuity provided by a soon-

[6] Jay Prosser, *Second Skins: The Body Narratives of Transsexuality* (New York: Columbia University Press, 1998), 5.

to-be familiar ukulele and drumbeat.[7] This framing is literalized above and below the opening frames by tapa-style borders cut from the same cloth as the backdrop to the title frame. The voice-over that introduces the documentary and directs our viewing similarly establishes the priority of culture over sex: "*Fa'afafine.* It means to be like a woman and Western labels like transvestite, transsexual, or gay just don't fit. Genetically and physically, *fa'afafine* are men. In their hearts, they're women and most want a long-term relationship with a heterosexual man." The voice-over confidently dismisses the relevance of terms such as "transvestite, transsexual, or gay" to Samoan sexual conduct while referencing a heterosexuality assumed to be transparent, the logical consequence of gender difference. By explicitly banishing other Western categories of sexual identity from its frame of understanding, *Queens of Samoa* nonetheless guarantees their secret return. Negated in these opening moments, homosexuality, in particular, haunts the documentary's representational strategies as the open secret of contemporary Samoan culture. That is, despite the forcefulness with which it says the opposite, the distinction between heterosexuality and homosexuality remains the defining categorical opposition for the documentary. This distinction allows the holistic segregation of Polynesian and European whereas if the difference represented by *fa'afafine* were allowed to resonate more widely, that distinction might lose the definitional hold it currently enjoys.

Although *Queens of Samoa* starts with an explicit statement about the mobility of gender inscription, that statement is uttered by a voice that is unambiguously female. Without giving it a thought, the viewer knows that voice to be a woman's. This is an important point in a documentary that foregrounds the slipperiness of gender transitivity and implies that unlike the Samoan culture that is being represented, the

---

[7] The term *Samoanicity* is modeled on Roland Barthes's coinage *Italianicity* to refer to a fantasy of Italianness, a hyperrepresentation without anchor in the banal truths of geography or nationality. *Image, Music, Text,* trans. Stephen Heath (New York: Hill and Wang, 1977), 33. Of course, the substantial body of literature on the reification of tradition in Samoa and the Pacific might be referenced here, but Barthes's discussion of the capacity of an image of some pasta and a few fresh vegetables to signify Italy is more in keeping with the shortened circuit of reference invoked in the title sequence.

Western culture that represents it has an uncomplicated relationship to gender. Naturally marked male or female, Westerners are secure in their gender, buffered against liminality's pull. Likewise, the cultural location of that voice-over is not without interest, precisely because the documentary avows no interest in it. The voice-over—its intonations, its vowels, its straining after but falling short of class neutrality—is recognizably that of a New Zealander, or *palāgi*. Not unaccented, then, the voice is nevertheless speaking its mother tongue. The voice-over maps out a home turf on which many subsequent voices, marked with Samoan accents and negotiating English as a second language, find themselves in the wrong neighborhood.

Although it is the lone *palāgi* voice, the voice-over enjoys a privilege that exceeds even its facility in English. Occasionally serving as a sound bridge between visual sequences—as do other, Samoan voices—the voice-over is far more than a continuity device: at times it approaches omniscience as a controlling narration. We never learn anything more about the voice; we never see who is talking—nor, perhaps, should we, because within the documentary the voice-over is the acoustic trace of an authorial or editorial function. The viewer identifies with the voice-over but only insofar as it represents a system of knowledge or intelligence. It would be a mistake to personalize it, to think of the warm throat from which it emanates before it is caught by the film's audio system. Rather, we need to consider how the voice-over is conflated with the technology that records both sound and visual images. As we watch and listen, we identify with the technology that controls visibility—who is seen and how—as the intelligence system that determines the documentary's meaningfulness. The feminine *palāgi* voice, then, is a blind. It naturalizes or personalizes that surveilling technology in a minimal way because to mark that voice too idiosyncratically would ruin the illusion of the documentary. Distracted by the specificities of that voice—who is she, and why is she saying these things about Samoan culture?—the viewer might slide out from under the weight of the structures of authority that the voice-over puts in place. As it is, that level, respectful, female voice maintains a seamlessness between the unseen technology that controls the meanings generated by the editing and sequencing of events and revelations and the Samoan voices to which it appears always to defer.

Witness

Having rejected the "labels" *transvestite, transsexual,* and *gay* as irrelevant, the documentary efficiently sets up the axes on which *fa'afafine* are to be located via autobiographical statements by Samoans who identify themselves as *fa'afafine.* In less than ten minutes, before the first commercial break, alternative indigenous definitional charts are in place, and their locating references are gendered and familial rather than sexual. The remaining forty minutes of screen time merely refine those coordinates over visuals that variously capture *fa'afafine* in the alternating locations of Apia and Auckland. The personal statements provided by these *fa'afafine* emphasize that they are to be understood through a gender-inversion model of human behavior, whether it is thought of solely as an inversion of the soul or mind, whether it is projected onto the surface of the body and its openings or onto the clothes that the body wears, or indeed whether any combination of these strategies is used. Self-fashioning, we learn, is particular to each *fa'afafine,* and there is no reason to assume that an individual feels the need to be consistent in this regard over his entire lifetime or to assume that he doesn't.

For example, Karl Pulotu-Endemann, a non-cross-dressing *fa'afafine,* asserts, "I'm very proud of who I am and I don't need to put on dresses to be that person. The most important thing to me is the thinking and your relationship to your family and your culture." Immediately after this personal testimony Fanafi Le Tagaloa gives her professorial analysis: "I think the *palāgi* view tends to polarise things. It must be very difficult for them to see the outward signs of an effeminate man and accept that this is a different being moving in a completely different world than an effeminate man moving in the Western world." These ideas about *fa'afafine* seem to proceed from Samoan culture itself via the privileged testimony of these two commentators. Of those on screen who identify themselves as *fa'afafine,* Pulotu-Endemann is the most articulate and reflective; the others sound more or less stilted in what is obviously their second language, English. A pattern is established whereby Pulotu-Endemann says something that is then repeated or elaborated by the Samoan academic or by the voice-over, so that whatever Pulotu-Endemann has said gains authority independently of its status as a personal reflection. Whereas most of the statements from the Samoans who think of themselves as *fa'afafine* remain autobiographical and so are truthful to themselves, Pulotu-Endemann's utterances accrue a kind of truthfulness cut loose from or in excess of that of witness.

Family

After the first commercial break the *palāgi* voice-over immediately reorients the viewer, restating and amplifying what Pulotu-Endemann and Le Tagaloa have already told us, that *fa'afafine*, howsoever they present, are always to be understood in relation to the family: "The heartbeat of Samoan society is the family. Historically *fa'afafine* always had a special place here." The documentary's point of view is sutured with the one ascribed to its privileged informant as the voice-over becomes Pulotu-Endemann's, although it takes a while for the viewer to realize who is talking, since the images reeling past signal no transition. The visual images bridge the different vocalizations as though there was no shift at all: the perspective is continuous, the insider knowledge now the property of the outside observer. Pulotu-Endemann, in his turn, reinforces what the *palāgi* voice-over has just said: "I can't think of any *āiga* or any extended family in Samoa that does not have a *fa'afafine*. We have existed in the Pacific for hundreds of years. The Samoan culture nurtured us. We were born *fa'afafine*, and we were nurtured by the culture and our families. That's what makes us special." However, this accommodation of gender-variant behavior by traditional Samoan institutions is overshadowed by the intolerance of Alex Futu, an Apian resident who, in accordance with his Christian faith, would like to send all *fa'afafine*—including, presumably, his gender-liminal son, Benji—into leper-like exile on some other island: "We can't sort of desert them to another island or something like that. I wish we could do that, but having *fa'afafine* around Samoa is a very sad thing to see." As Futu continues to speak, the camera turns to Benji, who is applying his makeup, and to the young figure crouched in the doorway, as mesmerized by Benji's image as Benji is himself. Throughout the scene the viewer is braced to resist not what is seen—Benji at the mirror, already skilled in the ways of *fa'afafine*, and the other boy clearly entranced by the spectacle—but what is heard, what Benji's father says in the name of Christianity: "First, I like a man to do what a man has to do. Get himself a wife, have children like myself and build up the family."

Having given voice to Benji's father, the documentary restores its alternative reading of *fa'afafine* by returning to Pulotu-Endemann, who guides our response to the revilement and denial of the youthful *fa'afafine* by his own family. Such a reaction is, Pulotu-Endemann lets us know, the consequence of the coming of Christianity to the Pacific and the declension of traditional Samoan culture; it is part of the damaging aftermath of contact. *Fa'afafine,* when neglected or rejected by their *āiga,* suffer isolation and loss of identity and, "in order to survive," found constellations of alternative families. Pulotu-Endemann's statement is confirmed when the documentary returns us to Auckland and another *fa'afafine,* the handsomely mustached, single-earringed Niko Uili, who, speaking of his drag-queen friends companionably arrayed the length of his sofa, says, in appropriately broken English, "My family for now, this is my flatmates." Under the governing rubric of family, the sideways shift from the church-sanctioned domesticity of Apia to its metropolitan other, a shared flat held in the orbit of an urbanized, semiprofessionalized sex industry, is made to seem unworthy of remark. The documentary's multiple discourses promote a version of cultural contamination in which the injustice of colonization warps the world in which Benji must take his place, a home that no longer knows him as its own. At the same time, the documentary all but ignores the postcolonial trajectory through which Benji's difference as an adult will probably find greater accommodation in the sexual subcultures of Auckland, Sydney, or Los Angeles than his home culture of Apia.

Visual Erotics

Although *Queens of Samoa* repeatedly insists that nineteenth-century missionaries, however well intended, were implicated in circuits of sexual projection and incitement, the documentary never acknowledges that it too might be entangled in such representational dynamics. Instead, it relies on the ethnographic conceit of the innocent observational gaze, a conceit given the lie in the scene described previously in which the figure of Benji is visually recruited to an editorial system that works less than transparently. Throughout the scene in which Benji's father speaks against *fa'afafine,* the camera is magnetized by the gender-liminal adolescent before the mirror and by the younger figure spying on him. The camera work links the figures of Benji and the other boy, allowing the significance of that connection to emerge without being spoken. Perhaps the sequence is intended to suggest the attraction of gender liminality, and what the camera records and conveys is the erotic, albeit low-voltage, charge conducted between the two boys. It is more plausible, however, to consider that the reflective camera work, which opens a contemplative gap between the image and the audio track, reveals that the effeminacy of *fa'afafine* is integral to the Western representational discourse that frames them as sexual other.

Whatever the linking of Benji and the other boy may tell us about the visual erotics of being or becoming *fa'afafine,* it undeniably reveals something about the visual politics of the documentary and its gendering. The camera's relationship to visibility is on display in this scene, not Benji's and not the younger boy's. Despite the moral burden carried by the soundtrack of Benji's father, the last word belongs to the image. The camera, in a prototypical gesture, opens up a discursive entry point for the viewer, who, receiving aural and visual informations that play against each other, makes a judgment between them. At this moment the viewer might be said to hold more knowledge than the Samoan participants. This scene exposes the ruse of a documentary that everywhere seems to defer to its informants in the matter of gendered identities. The structure of address embedded in the documentary thus becomes apparent insofar as the vulnerability of the youthful *fa'afafine* confirms the greater sexual understanding, the greater sexual sympathy, of the implied audience, and this more sophisticated sexual knowledge is gained by projecting a sexual innocence—here an ignorance—on to its off-screen Samoan interlocuter. This sexual knowledge is a function of the representational apparatus, never the property of those who stand before it.

If the sexually unmarked viewer has an identificatory relation to this reflective camera, the Samoan subjects do not or, at least, are not intended to. The documentary, however, contains several luminous moments in which the subjects do reveal such a relation to the camera and, in so doing, cloud its calmly diagnostic lens. These moments are all of a similar kind: some figure—sometimes *fa'afafine,* some-

times not; often a child, never the stern professor of Samoan studies—
while doing something, perhaps moving across the screen but saying
nothing, suddenly or slowly looks straight at the camera until a smile
breaks over his or her face that seems to take the camera at its word,
asking it to deliver on its promise of visual recognition. These engaging moments, which are cut loose from the voice-over, mark the point
at which subject and viewer are sutured into a spectatorial contract
that rides over the distinctions insisted on by the documentary. They
rupture the smooth operation of the documentary's structure of address that would otherwise keep its Samoan subjects and *palāgi* audience at arm's length.

Sexuality and Gender Inversion

Femininity is conferred on *fa'afafine* in two registers. First, in the
visual circuitry of the documentary the camera bestows an imaginary
recognition on the *fa'afafine* who perform before it, confirming their
attractiveness within an apparatus it has become second nature to describe as phallic. Second, their claim to femininity is corroborated
through the personalized connections that constitute the Samoan
family. Both registers, filmic and familial, underwrite a gender-inversion model of identity formation through which we are instructed to
understand *fa'afafine* as women trapped in the bodies of men, but we
should hardly need reminding that gender does not have a straightforward relation to representation, least of all to the representation of
sexuality. In any instance, it remains to be seen what the relation of
gender, gender inversion, and sexuality will be.

According to Bradd Shore, for example, the Samoan institution of
fa'afafine has traditionally been relied on to brace a gendered politics
of fertility and descent. Shore argues that gender inversion maintains
kinship categories essential to the tracings of genealogy, a practice
central to the social and political organization of Samoan life, just as
the dispensations allowed *fa'afafine* and their sexual partners pertain
to the prohibitions surrounding the sexual conduct of young women.[8]

[8] Bradd Shore, "Sexuality and Gender in Samoa: Conceptions and Misconceptions," in *Sexual Meanings: The Cultural Construction of Gender and Sexuality*, ed.
Sherry B. Ortner and Harriet Whitehead (Cambridge: Cambridge University Press,
1981), 192–215.

Jeanette-Marie Mageo agrees that in the Samoan instance gender inversion needs to be understood in relation to kinship structures rather than a privatized sphere of sexual motivation, but in a departure from Shore, she argues that gender liminality "mitigates" otherwise unstable gender differentials between males and females. The phenomenon of *fa'afafine* "occurs where gender binarism is unstable and is then exploited by cultural members to maintain gender binarism," which is why, Mageo argues, male transvestism is increasingly prevalent in modern Samoan culture; it functions prophylactically, reinforcing "gender polarities when they are under siege," as they have been since the "relative feminization of male roles that missionization provoked."[9] In an earlier article Mageo discusses the ironic modes of self-representation employed by *fa'afafine* and their role in deflecting erotic tension away from relations between young Samoan males and unmarried girls. Once again, Mageo's argument reveals that the gender liminality of *fa'afafine* can have a conservative function in relation to the compulsory regimes of heterosexuality, from which it is an apparent departure.[10]

This anthropological work establishes that the relation between gender liminality and sexuality, either homosexual or heterosexual, can never be taken for granted. Precisely because the tropes of gender are understood to articulate not only heterosexuality but the homosexuality from which it stands apart, the instance of gender liminality that *fa'afafine* embody crucially feeds into that bifurcated representational economy. The liminal identities of *fa'afafine*, insofar as they both comply with and abuse the rules of gender, always threaten to disrupt the heterosexual and homosexual economies that are founded on those rules. In order to keep intact its sexual certainties, *Queens of Samoa* must work hard to prevent this dissonance from emerging. The chief defense it employs to maintain the separation between *fa'afafine* and Western sexual identities is an apparent refusal to inquire into sexual relations. Although at times it flirts with an explicitness about sexual matters—"whether they dress as women for fun or are serious about it, *fa'afafine* are quite clear about who they're at-

---

[9] Jeanette-Marie Mageo, "Samoa, on the Wilde Side: Male Transvestism, Oscar Wilde, and Liminality in Making Gender," *Ethos* 24, no. 4 (1996): 610, 592.

[10] Jeanette-Marie Mageo, "Male Transvestism and Cultural Change in Samoa," *American Ethnologist* 19, no. 3 (1992): 443–59.

tracted to"—the documentary always returns to a coyness about sex and never shows *fa'afafine* in activities beyond the putting on of makeup or an exaggerated primping at an unseen audience. Questions about sexual gratification threaten to arise in the responses of *fa'afafine* who are asked whether or not they want to undergo sex-change operations, but in the documentary's ordering of these responses the subject of pleasure is quickly eclipsed by talk of family responsibilities and the care of children. It's not about sex; it's about family.

The celebrated inclusiveness of the Samoan family is thrown into relief, however, by the exclusiveness of the Samoan church. A Pacific Island Church minister describes his New Zealand Samoan congregation's relationship to *fa'afafine:* "They understand the niceties of the term, but when it comes down to the actual sexual activity, I think that is an area some of our people would not want to delve into." As if in response, the next subject, an unnamed *fa'afafine,* explains that the Samoan church's prejudice is based on a misunderstanding. *Fa'afafine,* he states, are mistaken as homosexual and thus taken to violate a biblical prohibition, but in his own understanding of himself gender does not correspond to sex, so his relations with men are with opposites to himself. Thus, his desires are heterosexual insofar as they are incited by a difference in sexual ascription. Pulotu-Endemann also claims that missionaries misrecognized *fa'afafine* as men and thus condemned their sexual activities as sodomy.[11]

In contradistinction to the impulse to see sin and homosexuality everywhere, the gender-inversion understanding of *fa'afafine* that the documentary elaborates preserves the heterosexuality of desire: only opposites attract, as if difference were the engine of desire. The documentary, which seems to be a relaxed or liberal account of how anything goes genderwise, mobilizes an inversion model of sexual identity ("a woman's soul in a man's body") in what Judith Butler,

---

[11] There is little evidence for Pulotu-Endemann's claim. The nineteenth-century missionary archives, preoccupied as they are with sexual conduct, are startlingly silent on the phenomenon of *fa'afafine.* See Mageo, "Samoa," 588–89. Besnier also comments on the discrepancy between "the copious early accounts of *māhū* in Tahiti, and, more equivocally, of comparable categories in Hawaii, the Marquesas and New Zealand" and the lack of reference to "the phenomenon in Western Polynesia, despite the fact that it is equally conspicuous in all regions today." Besnier, "Polynesian Gender Liminality," 294.

writing of drag, calls "the service of both the denaturalisation and reidealisation of hyperbolic gender norms."[12] *Queens of Samoa* denaturalizes femininity and masculinity only to reassert the compulsory heterosexuality of desire. Via the gesture of accommodating difference, it thus shores up, at a stroke, both the family and the heterosexuality from which it derives. This fetishization of gender, furthermore, can be instantiated by *fa'afafine* only to the degree that they are dematerialized, that is, to the degree that they are denied any narrative of sexual embodiment. The documentary patently manifests no interest in the sex *fa'afafine* have or who they have it with, and the strict maintenance of that disinterest keeps unassailable the contention that there is no synonymity between *fa'afafine* and nonindigenous sexual categories. The ideological coherence of gender sustains the fantasy that *fa'afafine* is a hermetically sealed traditional category impervious to historical change.

Kinship

Queens of Samoa refuses to pursue any contradiction that is not finally retrievable to a version of colonial abuse. In this way it avoids offending any of its imagined audiences except, perhaps, the gay and transgender ones. The privileged narrative it tells remains first of all the tragedy of contact with its corroding of the traditional Samoan way. This foundational tragedy then dovetails, in the twentieth century, with the tragedy of migration and the scattering of the Samoan population across the metropolitan centers of the Pacific Rim. Because of that scattering, the documentary goes on to demonstrate, *fa'afafine* are exposed like other Polynesian migrants to the violence of racism and, further, to the indignity of an inappropriate—because misdirected—homophobic discrimination.

The bleakness of this double tragedy is attested to later when the *fa'afafine* dream of the longtime heterosexual companion is dispelled by the reality of living alone. However brief their term, no partners are ever seen in *Queens of Samoa*, so the impression we are given is that the *fa'afafine* longing for a male heterosexual partner is completely

---

[12] Judith Butler, *Bodies That Matter: On the Discursive Limits of "Sex"* (New York: Routledge, 1993), 125.

wishful, a fantasy indulged in the face of stark reality. Returning to the emptiness of his Auckland flat, a *fa'afafine* recounts his family's proliferation, thereby mapping an expansion that leaves him alone: "When we first came here, we were all living together, one family, brothers and sisters, but they've all gone out and married and have their own houses and that. I prefer living alone and, uh, I had a relationship one time for a couple of years and that's it, that's about the only, uh, the longest relationship I had. I rather stay by myself." The shaping of the end of the documentary restates and resecures the idea that New Zealand culture erodes the Samoan family and at best (or worst) replaces it with a transgender culture that may or may not open onto a gay scene. The relationships desired by these *fa'afafine* inevitably fail. Abandoned, they are isolated, lost to their families and lost between two worlds. What the documentary offers as compensation is the return to Apia and a culture that claims them as kin. Referring to a ball staged for *fa'afafine* at an island resort hotel, Le Tagaloa says, "All the family . . . turn up to support [them] not because they are competing as drag queens but because he [i.e., they] happens to be my cousin, my son, my brother. Whether we like or support what they are doing. That is the kind of society we have." The magnetic pull of this familial culture is represented as strong enough to hold even the alien as its own. Thus the American-derived beauty pageant in Apia is a "uniquely Samoan festival."

In this documentary Samoa is the family. The colonial story *Queens of Samoa* tells is that the family that once nurtured difference was damaged through contact and now, in the name of Christianity, rejects its own. The remedy it prescribes for the family's insufficiencies is more family. This is achieved via the restoration of kinship categories: *fa'afafine* are "our brothers and sons." What *Queens of Samoa* ends with, in the person of the physically diminutive but symbolically huge professor of Samoan studies, is the matriarchal gathering of *fa'afafine* (the gender inverts) into the unproblematically gendered positions they occupy in that kinship system. That, apparently, has never been in question: no one has ever taken *fa'afafine* to be their sisters or daughters.

Such is the Samoan way in Apia, but in the Samoan diaspora, family threatens to become dystopian. We might remark here one of the representations of Samoanness that circulates easily in New Zealand editorial culture: Samoa equals family, and under the lightest pressure the equation yields a series of metonyms; family can be made contiguous with domestic violence, sexual abuse, welfare fraud. *Queens of Samoa* does not do that, but it does offer the formulation—although the analysis seemingly proceeds from inside that culture, as if it were not observations made about Samoans but insider knowledge that informants have let us share—that the Samoan *āiga*, once transported to New Zealand, is replaced by the pretended family. The culmination of this narrative trajectory as the documentary arranges it is a sad one: a Samoan living in an empty flat, no longtime companion, family long gone. This is the tragic narrative of cultural estrangement. The gender in-between now falls between two worlds—no one's son, no one's brother—and the deprivation endured in that state beyond kinship is underlined by the final switch to Le Tagaloa and the festive Apia scene, which celebrates, if nothing else, the cultural heft of family.

The extended family becomes the pretended family most obviously in the Auckland-based pseudofamily comprised of Uili and his drag-queen flatmates. Uili, a sometime drag artiste but otherwise mustached, earringed man, calls these companions his "for now" family, but he also states that he has not told his other family, which is still in Western Samoa, that he is *fa'afafine*. This revelation is telling because in the logic of the documentary, *fa'afafine*, as a gendered identity, never needs disclosing, least of all to the Samoan family from which it traditionally derives. Uili's revelation that he is a closeted or secret *fa'afafine* suggests an opacity to this category that the documentary cannot engage. Nor is there anything about Uili's presentation to the camera that suggests effeminacy. Insofar as Uili knows something about himself that he has yet to tell his relatives, his identification as *fa'afafine* appears to have the structure of an identity— even a sexuality—that must be claimed or avowed rather than simply read off from him. Uili's sexual personhood arises on the seam between two overlapping cultures, and for him that doubling is productive of an identity, not corrosive of one. Though Uili's recognition of himself as *fa'afafine* makes sense in the gay and transgender culture of Auckland, his reluctance to tell his family suggests that that same identification would cause agitation in Samoa. Far from being discontinuous, indigenous and nonindigenous understandings converge, and Uili, like other *fa'afafine*, must negotiate that convergence and its crosswise transversal of space.

Secrecy

The distinction between *fa'afafine* and homosexuality, transvestism, and transsexuality is nowhere as stable as *Queens of Samoa* would have us believe. Rather, the documentary attests to the necessary enforcement of that treacherous distinction. This is not to say that the contemporary Pacific is an intolerant place. It is a tolerant place, and its inhabitants are all contained in regimes of tolerance, although differently. *Fa'afafine,* for instance, are tolerated insofar as they are not embodied sexual subjects, although the only voice reckless enough to say as much in this documentary belongs to the New Zealand–born Pacific Island Church minister.[13] The cultural spaces in which the difference between *fa'afafine* and those other sexual identities is articulated include both gay and non-gay locations. Despite the voice-over's assurance that *fa'afafine* have "no doubt about who they are attracted to," who finds *fa'afafine* attractive goes unspoken. Wherever those encounters occur, *Queens of Samoa* has an investment in keeping them enigmatic. That not-saying is as powerful as saying, and what it puts in place is the idea that Samoan culture keeps a secret: not the secret of gender inversion, an idealized version of heterosexual maintenance and thus no secret at all, but the secret of sex, of whom *fa'afafine* are going with.

Furthermore, *Queens of Samoa* keeps that secret inadequately. It is as if the too insistent flagging of heterosexual affiliation installs the suspicion of its opposite. That epistemological maneuver is recognizably colonialist; it projects the compulsory ordering of Western culture onto Samoa, making sexuality the privileged secret of Samoans, as it is ours. Thus the recognition that *Queens of Samoa* conveys is doubly dubious. In refusing to allow any meaningful continuity between *fa'afafine* and Western categories of sexual identification, it

---

[13] Despite its often self-congratulatory poise, tolerance can be more heavy-handed than prejudice. Consider, for example, Jan Cameron's discussion of the reactions of Auckland netball administrators to the 1994 decision of the New Zealand Netball Federation "to sex-test players who might be transvestites without breaching privacy and human rights laws." Sensitive to the intensive Pacific Island involvement in the sport—and consequently, to the likelihood of *fa'afafine* involvement in it—Auckland administrators urged netball teams to be self-surveilling and to enroll in mixed (men's and women's) competition if there was any doubt as to the gender identity of their members. "For Women's Own Good: Gender Verification of Female Athletes," *Women's Studies Journal* 12, no. 1 (1996): 8.

seemingly says nothing about sexuality while speaking of nothing else. It effectively elides *fa'afafine* with all it says they are not. The relationship between sexual concealment and sexual disclosure is never straightforward, but to avoid the structuring logic of denial, the makers of this documentary would have had to perform the more difficult act of addressing its complicity with those mechanisms of sexual representation.[14] Wittingly or unwittingly, *Queens of Samoa* charts, as effectively as Cook's voyages, the Pacific space many of us now call home, marked as it continues to be with an intermittent knowingness concerning sexual relations between men.

The animating gesture of *Queens of Samoa* is to insist on the historical discontinuity of *fa'afafine* and homosexuality, but insofar as that turning toward the traditional is simultaneously a turning away from the necessity and risk of the present, the gesture might be thought negligent. The documentary's thesis of cultural and sexual relativism—its bracketing of *fa'afafine* as distinct from homosexuals, transvestites, and transsexuals—coupled with its feigned indifference to the sexual activities of gender-liminal Polynesians and the sexual and ethnic registration of their partners (gay or straight, European or Samoan) works to deny or erase continuities between cultures. This erasure has deadly consequence in a Pacific location such as the one from which I write, where young Polynesian men who identify themselves across gender and not as gay are the population most vulnerable to HIV infection and most beyond the reach of preventative education programs.[15] The viral transmission of AIDS does not respect the semantic difference between *fa'afafine* and gay, transvestite, or transsexual. As is evidenced in the public health tracking of the epidemic, HIV continues to infect across different embodiments of sex. This is not to say that we must, under the urgent imperative of AIDS—

---

[14] The question of who has sex with *fa'afafine* is a highly charged one in many contexts. I do not deny that documentary makers and, increasingly, ethnographers in countries such as Western Samoa are subject to government approval concerning what they can and cannot depict. Censorship, however, is the devil we know; I am more concerned with the representational mechanisms of a benign tolerance that underwrites not just *Queens of Samoa* but many ostensibly gay-friendly portrayals of same-sex sexuality. It is the apparent transparency of the more sophisticated, less prohibitive gesture that I question.

[15] This was the finding of a study undertaken by the New Zealand AIDS Foundation. *Needs Assessment: Pacific Islands Men Who Have Sex with Men*, New Zealand AIDS Foundation Report to North Health, November 1996.

its discursive no less than its epidemiological effects—ride roughshod over the niceties of cultural differentiation to install "homosexuality" as a universally legible rubric, but to recognize that some of the most efficacious and rigorous distinctions between sexual identities and the sexual acts with which they are all too often assumed to be cognate are being made in AIDS education and policy work.[16]

What the documentary reveals is the remarkable ease with which the crucial lesson that there are distinctions to be made between Polynesian and European sexual behaviors—a lesson that could unsettle much widely held knowledge about gender and sexuality, sexual behavior and sexual identity—can be not only learned by heart but used to safeguard the very complacencies it might be understood to challenge. In *Queens of Samoa* the ready disavowal of homosexual continuities in the name of Polynesian difference does not disarticulate the enmeshed fields of gender and sexuality but recuperates gender liminality in the service of a heterosexual hegemony that, unlike its homosexual counterpart, is taken to be culturally universal. The heterosexual metaphorization of the Pacific, it seems, is as sustainable now as it was in the eighteenth century.

[16] For other regionally specific instances of such work, see Michael Bartos, John McLeod, and Phil Nott, *Meanings of Sex between Men: A Study Conducted by the Australian Federation of AIDS Organisations for the Commonwealth Department of Human Services and Health* (Canberra: Australian Government Publishing Service, 1993); Gary Dowsett, *Men Who Have Sex with Men: National HIV/AIDS Education* (Canberra: Australian Government Publishing Service, 1991); *Sexual Cultures and Migration in the Era of AIDS: Anthropological and Demographic Perspectives*, ed. Gilbert Herdt (Oxford: Clarendon Press, 1997); and Heather Worth, "Up on K Road on a Saturday Night: Sex, Gender, and Sex Work in Auckland," *Venereology: The Interdisciplinary, International Journal of Sexual Health* 13, no. 1 (2000): 15–24.

Conclusion

In the document that will become almost definitive of modern anthropology's agonized relation to cultural difference and sexual expression, Bronislaw Malinowski records a dream he had while living among the Trobriand Islanders:

> Today, Monday, 9.20.14, I had a strange dream; homosex., with my own double as partner. Strangely autoerotic feelings; the impression that I'd like to have a mouth just like mine to kiss, a neck that curves just like mine, a forehead just like mine (seen from the side). I got up tired and collected myself slowly.[1]

Malinowski's dream is highly suggestive, less for the subconscious it opens onto than the ethnographic field in which it occurs. If in this conclusion I recall these dream notations that catch at the half-truths of sleep, it is in the hope that they might critically dislodge other, less reflexive dreamings of the Pacific in which the relation between heterosexual agent and homosexual subtext is less openly displayed.[2]

---

[1] Bronislaw Malinowski, *A Diary in the Strict Sense of the Term* (Routledge and Kegan Paul, 1967; reprint, intro. Raymond Firth, Stanford: Stanford University Press, 1989), 12–13.

[2] The Pacific has frequently been organized via the trope of dreaming or fantasy, the enactment of which inevitably falls short of these imaginings and delivers the dreamer to an unpremeditated experience. See, for example, Gavan Daws's book on

The project of this book has been to reopen the Pacific to sexual imagining. Comprising a series of readings of cross-cultural encounters—from Cook's voyages to the recent documentary *Fa'afafine: Queens of Samoa*—it argues that the critical categories that have been used to interpret forms of same-sex desire in native contexts have been inadequate to the complex transformational effects precipitated by those encounters on both parties. Whether to celebrate or condemn, most accounts of Pacific sexual contact assume the heterosexual profile of that exchange. Against this assumption, this book has advanced a homosexual template for thinking about the transactional grammar of Pacific sexual representation. It has purposely stressed the homosexual with as much hyperbole as has previously attached to the heterosexual, not simply to expose some of the muffled thinking that dogs writing about sexual encounter but to demonstrate that many of our modern understandings of sexuality were conceived through Pacific ethnography. Our contemporary delineations of sexual identity, from the most casual to the most exact, involve a tangled inheritance that reaches from the present back through the archives of Pacific encounter to their beginning in the eighteenth century.

Throughout this book I have deployed two axes of translation: between European and Polynesian constructions of gender and sexuality, and between past and present epochs. Whether analyzing originary documents of cross-cultural encounter or their critical commentary, I have drawn attention to the way the sexualization of both other places and past times can be narrativized to bolster ethnocentric and presentist claims. No direct approach to the past can avoid these outcomes and effects, so I have used a range of provisional reading strategies and critical methodologies to maintain the diacritical relation between those four terms: European and Polynesian, past and present. It is always problematic, for instance, to reimagine prior indigenous sexual regimes through the records of past travelers. This book makes the theoretical assumption that within the European archive of Pacific contact, cross-cultural sexual recognition more often appears in the opacity of reported events than the illusory lucidity of textual interpretation. Thus these readings more often fasten on what goes unsaid in encounter, or what fails to draw remark, than on

---

Pacific residency: *A Dream of Islands: Voyages of Self-Discovery in the South Seas* (Milton, Queensland: Jacaranda Press, 1980).

the interpretative systems that are being put in place in order to render Polynesian cultures and their sexual systems symbolically transparent or understandable. By interrogating this archive for signs of sexual opacity—such as that indexed by the failure of Cook's officers to respond to Hawaiian male solicitation—these readings retroactively deduce from such blind spots a sexual incoherence on which imperial ideology then gets a grip. Similarly, the interpretative interventions of this book have strategically focused on understandings of historical events—the expulsion of William Yate from the ranks of the Church Missionary Society for sexual misdemeanors, for example—which are now canonical in order to unsettle those sedimented readings and the ancillary ideological effects that attach to them. When both original event and subsequent commentary are placed in previously unexamined contexts, the premature assumption of sexual orthodoxies is precluded. Instead, incident and commentary are made newly accountable to both a past and a present moment and to the different sexual agents those moments implicate. This strategy reveals that the charged distinction between homosexual and heterosexual is always a product of these historical events and debates, not simply their precondition.

Rather than assert a new Pacific canon against a traditional one, the interpretative tactic of *Sexual Encounters* has been to listen for an internal dissidence that has always resonated within the privileged texts of the Pacific. Prior reading on sexual exchange within the Pacific ethnographic and literary archive has favored the female body over the male, the heterosexual over the nascently homosexual, yet that same canon can be made to yield an alternate emphasis. For the lionized texts of James Cook and Joseph Banks, Herman Melville and Paul Gauguin demonstrably figure an alternate tradition that is less securely mortgaged to the expression of heterosexuality. However, this skewing of the Pacific canon is not done in order to produce a counterorthodoxy of a gay Pacific. The last thing *Sexual Encounters* is intended to inaugurate is a fantasy of the Pacific as the site of homosexual abandon. Rather, the book's critical reimagining of the Pacific remains the best strategy for avoiding the now ubiquitous opposition between the heterosexual and the homosexual. This rhetorical appropriation of the Pacific crystallizes the two-way operation of my argument. For it is not simply that the categories of sexual identity we now hold as our own have particular and traceable histories, but also that identifying those histories may dislodge the inevitability of the sexual present. The past, then, is not simply the back-projection of the present but the point of its unraveling. If *Sexual Encounters* stresses the entanglement of both European and Polynesian regimes of sexuality, it is in order to demonstrate the extent to which that mutually transformative process is still under way, its outcomes still fully contestable. In order to preserve the openness of that outcome, the assertion of the dual historical profile of such processes—their animation in both past and present—must be augmented by a "double vision" that simultaneously deploys the lens of indigenous and European, female and male, homo- and heterocentric perspectives on those interactions.[3]

The readings that comprise this book could do worse than take as their emblem an image by the contemporary gay artists Pierre and Gilles which luminously condenses many of my theoretical arguments. *Saint Pierre Marie Chanel* (unavailable for black-and-white reproduction) is modeled on a thousand classical depositions of Christ. In the pink-hibiscus-framed scene, the kneeling priest, Chanel, is administering last rites to a young native man dying from a beautiful wound in his side on some B-grade beach. The dark-skinned model could be North African, but the iconography is undoubtedly Pacific, juxtaposing as it does the upright missionary and the recumbent native, the clerical cloth and the *pareu*. This faux-Pacific image constitutes a vernacular shorthand for a recognizable sexuality. Equally handsome, the two male models articulate between them a cliché of gay eroticism, the charge of which is carried not only by them and their staged relation but also by the Pacific mise-en-scène. The aes-

---

[3] Nicholas Thomas has coined the term *double vision*, which reverberates against *European vision*, in order to suggest the critical shift undergone in Pacific art history since the field was founded by Bernard Smith. Thomas is promoting a dual attentiveness in art criticism to both European and indigenous aesthetic traditions, but I suspect he also has in mind Greg Dening's parable of the "double helix" for thinking about the unstable correspondences between past and present. The double helix similarly poises ostensibly oppositional structures in productive interrelation. I extend both terms to include not just European and Polynesian, past and present, but also the dubiously bifurcated fields of gender and sexuality. Nicholas Thomas and Diane Losche, eds., *Double Vision: Art Histories and Colonial Histories in the Pacific* (Cambridge: Cambridge University Press, 1999), 1–5. Greg Dening, *Mr. Bligh's Bad Language: Passion, Power, and Theatre on the Bounty* (Cambridge: Cambridge University Press, 1992), 8–9.

thetic annexation of a historical Pacific repertoire for homosexual sig-nification should arrive, at this point in my argument, as the appro-priate rather than gratuitous outcome of two centuries of Pacific representation. *Sexual Encounters* has insisted on the historical cross-hatching of Pacific and European sexual discourses that both enables and restrains the modern category of homosexuality. Framed by an ar-tificial beach, the Technicolor scene Pierre and Gilles present aptly in-dexes an imagined South Seas moment from the perspective of a contemporary sexual identity which is that moment's legacy. Thus *Saint Pierre Marie Chanel* can be read not simply as a recuperation of a past Pacific moment for retroactive identification and the projec-tion of a counterhegemonic tradition—though it permits both those things—but as a historically motivated portrait that equally suggests that these possibilities or outcomes were enabled by the conjuncture of European and Polynesian sexual regimes in the first place.

Despite the manifest heterosexualization of the Pacific tradition, one of the outcomes of Pacific sexual encounter is that the term *het-erosexual* is always crossed by its other, the homosexual. However, to the degree that the insistent heterosexual ideology of the Pacific archive continues to be naturalized by its inheritors—as discretionary now as it was previously hegemonic—it is also befitting that *Sexual Encounters'* emblematic sexual scene be organized through the highly artificial aesthetic of kitsch. Decoratively excessive in the style of Pierre and Gilles, *Saint Pierre Marie Chanel* is entirely consistent with the artists' signature representations of hypericonic moments of romance and mortality. Although the illustration can yet raise a gasp in anthropological circles, the outrage centering on that complacent white hand resting on a *tapu* Polynesian head, when *Saint Pierre Marie Chanel* was exhibited in New Zealand in 1995, the image hung entirely innocuously in the Wellington City Gallery. Instead, all the scandal attached itself to *Glory Hole*, in which a tattooed young leatherman, his ecstatic face dripping with semen, grips a still erect penis.[4] The Wellington City Council thought *Glory Hole* best dis-played inside a private viewing booth, though in so doing it is unclear whether council members sought to diminish or amplify the eroticism of the image. Perhaps only in such company could Chanel's faux-

---

[4] See *Pierre et Gilles*, exhibition catalog, intro. Jonathan Turner (Sydney: Bloxham and Chambers, 1995).

Pacific ministrations go unremarked. If there is no longer any whiff of scandal surrounding such a homoerotic pose, it is nevertheless a reminder of how closely, under the rubric of the Pacific, run the tropes of seduction and conversion, pastoral and sexual attentions. A reminder, that is, of the diametrically opposed but intensely volatile relations that still connect European and Polynesian sexual identities, past and present sexual regimes.

Works Cited

Anderson, Benedict. *Imagined Communities: Reflections on the Origin and Spread of Nationalism.* London: Verso, 1983.

Barthes, Roland. *Image, Music, Text.* Trans. Stephen Heath. New York: Hill and Wang, 1977.

Bartos, Michael, John McLeod, and Phil Nott. *Meanings of Sex between Men: A Study Conducted by the Australian Federation of AIDS Organisations for the Commonwealth Department of Human Services and Health.* Canberra: Australian Government Publishing Service, 1993.

Beaglehole, J. C. *The Life of Captain James Cook.* Stanford: Stanford University Press, 1974.

——, ed. *The Endeavour Journal of Joseph Banks, 1768–1771.* 2 vols. Sydney: Trustees of the Public Library of New South Wales in association with Angus and Robertson, 1962.

——, ed. *The Journals of Captain James Cook on His Voyages of Discovery.* 4 vols. and a portfolio. London: Cambridge University Press for the Hakluyt Society, 1955–74.

Besnier, Niko. "Polynesian Gender Liminality through Time and Space." In *Third Sex, Third Gender: Beyond Dimorphism in Culture and History,* ed. Gilbert Herdt, 285–328. New York: Zone Books, 1994.

——. "Sluts and Superwomen: The Politics of Gender Liminality in Urban Tonga." *Ethnos* 62, nos. 1–2 (1997): 5–31.

Binney, Judith. Introduction to *An Account of New Zealand and of the Formation and Progress of the Church Missionary Society's Mission in the Northern Island,* by William Yate. 2d ed. 1835. Reprint, Wellington: A. H. and A. W. Reed, 1970.

——. *The Legacy of Guilt: A Life of Thomas Kendall.* Auckland: Oxford University Press, 1968.

———. Letter in response to Frank Sargeson's review of *An Account of New Zealand and of the Formation and Progress of the Church Missionary Society's Mission in the Northern Island,* by William Yate. *Landfall* 25, no. 4 (1971): 473–74.

———. "Whatever Happened to Poor Mr. Yate? An Exercise in Voyeurism." *New Zealand Journal of History* 9, no. 2 (1975): 110–25.

———. "William Yate." In *The Dictionary of New Zealand Biography:* Volume 1: *1769–1869,* ed. W. H. Oliver, 611–12. Wellington: Allen and Unwin for the Department of Internal Affairs, 1990.

Bleys, Rudi C. *The Geography of Perversion: Male-to-Male Sexual Behaviour outside the West and the Ethnographic Imagination, 1750–1918.* New York: New York University Press, 1995.

Bongie, Christopher. *Exotic Memories: Literature, Colonialism, and the Fin de Siècle.* Stanford: Stanford University Press, 1991.

Bougainville, Louis de. *A Voyage around the World.* Trans. John [Johann] Reinhold Forster. London: J. Nouse and T. Davies, 1772.

The Bounty. Dir. Roger Donaldson. De Laurentis, 1984.

Bray, Alan. *Homosexuality in Renaissance England.* London: Gay Men's Press, 1982.

Brettell, Richard. "Reclining Nude." Catalog Note 161. In *The Art of Paul Gauguin,* ed. Richard Brettell, Françoise Cachin, Claire Frèches-Thory, and Charles F. Stuckey, 308–9. Washington, D.C.: National Gallery of Art, 1988.

———. "The Return to France." In *The Art of Paul Gauguin,* ed. Richard Brettell, Françoise Cachin, Claire Frèches-Thory, and Charles F. Stuckey, 297–302. Washington, D.C.: National Gallery of Art, 1988.

Brooks, Peter. "Gauguin's Tahitian Body." *Yale Journal of Criticism* 3, no. 2 (1990): 51–89.

Butler, Judith. *Bodies That Matter: On the Discursive Limits of "Sex."* New York: Routledge, 1993.

Cachin, Françoise. "Self-Portrait with Hat (recto); Portrait of William Molard (verso)." Catalog Note 164. In *The Art of Paul Gauguin,* ed. Richard Brettell, Françoise Cachin, Claire Frèches-Thory, and Charles F. Stuckey, 311–13. Washington, D.C.: National Gallery of Art, 1988.

Cameron, Jan. "For Women's Own Good: Gender Verification of Female Athletes." *Women's Studies Journal* 12, no. 1 (1996): 7–24.

Carter, Harold B. *Sir Joseph Banks, 1743–1820.* London: British Museum, 1988.

Clark, T. J. *The Painting of Modern Life: Paris in the Art of Manet and His Followers.* Princeton: Princeton University Press, 1984.

Daws, Gavan. *A Dream of Islands: Voyages of Self-Discovery in the South Seas.* Milton, Queensland: Jacaranda Press, 1980.

Dening, Greg. *Islands and Beaches: Discourse on a Silent Land: Marquesas, 1774–1880.* Melbourne: Melbourne University Press, 1980.

———. *Mr. Bligh's Bad Language: Passion, Power, and Theatre on the Bounty.* Cambridge: Cambridge University Press, 1992.

——, ed. *The Marquesan Journal of Edward Robarts, 1797–1824.* Pacific History Series, no. 6. Canberra: Australian National University Press, 1974.

Diderot, Denis. *Political Writings.* Trans. and ed. John Hope Mason and Robert Wokler. Cambridge: Cambridge University Press, 1992.

Dowsett, Gary. *Men Who Have Sex with Men: National HIV/AIDS Education.* Canberra: Australian Government Publishing Service, 1991.

Edelman, Lee. *Homographesis: Essays in Gay Literary and Cultural Theory.* New York: Routledge, 1994.

Edmond, Rod. *Representing the South Pacific: Colonial Discourse from Cook to Gauguin.* Cambridge: Cambridge University Press, 1997.

——. "Translating Cultures: William Ellis and Missionary Writing." In *Science and Exploration in the Pacific: European Voyages to the Southern Oceans in the Eighteenth Century,* ed. Margarette Lincoln, 149–61. Woodbridge, Suffolk: Boydell Press in association with the National Maritime Museum, 1998.

Eisenman, Stephen F. *Gauguin's Skirt.* London: Thames and Hudson, 1997.

Ellis, William [surgeon's mate]. *An Authentic Narrative of a Voyage Performed by Captain Cook and Captain Clerke, in His Majesty's Ships Resolution and Discovery.* 2 vols. London: G. Robinson, J. Sewell, and J. Debrett, 1782.

Ellis, William [missionary]. *Polynesian Researches, during a Residence of Nearly Six Years in the South Sea Islands.* 2 vols. London: Fisher, 1829.

Elliston, Deborah A. "Erotic Anthropology: 'Ritualized Homosexuality' in Melanesia and Beyond." *American Ethnologist* 22 (1995): 848–67.

Fa'afafine: Queens of Samoa. Dir. Caroline Harker. Communicado, 1995.

Forster, George. *A Voyage round the World in His Britannic Majesty's Sloop, Resolution.* 2 vols. London: B. White, 1777.

Forster, John [Johann] Reinhold. *Observations Made during a Voyage round the World.* London: G. Robinson, 1778.

Foster, Hal. "'Primitive' Scenes." *Critical Inquiry* 20 (1993): 69–102.

Foucault, Michel. *The History of Sexuality,* vol. 1: *An Introduction.* Trans. Robert Hurley. New York: Pantheon, 1978.

Frèches-Thory, Claire. "Manao tupapau." Catalog note 154. In *The Art of Paul Gauguin,* ed. Richard Brettell, Françoise Cachin, Claire Frèches-Thory, and Charles F. Stuckey, 279–82. Washington, D.C.: National Gallery of Art, 1988.

Gauguin, Paul. *Noa Noa: Gauguin's Tahiti.* Ed. Nicholas Wadley. Trans. Jonathan Griffin. Oxford: Phaidon, 1985.

——. *The Writings of a Savage.* Ed. Daniel Guérin. Trans. Eleanor Levieux. New York: Viking Press, 1978.

Gell, Alfred. *Wrapping in Images: Tattooing in Polynesia.* Oxford: Clarendon Press, 1993.

Gilbert, Arthur N. "The *Africaine* Courts Martial: A Study of Buggery and the Royal Navy." *Journal of Homosexuality* 1 (1974): 111–22.

——. "Buggery and the British Navy, 1700–1861." *Journal of Social History* 10 (1976): 72–98.

Goldberg, Jonathan. *Sodometries: Renaissance Texts, Modern Sexualities.* Stanford: Stanford University Press, 1992.

Halperin, David M. "Forgetting Foucault: Acts, Identities, and the History of Sexuality." *Representations* 63 (1998): 93–120.

Hawkesworth, John. *An Account of the Voyages and Discoveries in the Southern Hemisphere.* 3 vols. London: W. Strahan and T. Cadell, 1773.

Hegarty, Neil. "Unruly Subjects: Sexuality, Science, and Discipline in Eighteenth-Century Pacific Exploration." In *Science and Exploration in the Pacific: European Voyages to the Southern Oceans in the Eighteenth Century,* ed. Margarette Lincoln, 183–97. Woodbridge, Suffolk: Boydell Press in association with the National Maritime Museum, 1998.

Herbert, T. Walter, Jr. *Marquesan Encounters: Melville and the Meaning of Civilization.* Cambridge: Harvard University Press, 1980.

Herdt, Gilbert. *Guardians of the Flutes: Idioms of Masculinity.* Chicago: University of Chicago Press, 1994.

——. "Representations of Homosexuality in Traditional Societies: An Essay on Cultural Ontology and Historical Comparison, Parts 1 and 2." *Journal of the History of Sexuality* 1, no. 3 (1991): 481–504; no. 4 (1991): 603–32.

——. *The Sambia: Ritual and Gender in New Guinea.* New York: Holt, Rinehart and Winston, 1987.

——, ed. *Ritualized Homosexuality in Melanesia.* Berkeley: University of California Press, 1984.

——, ed. *Sexual Cultures and Migration in the Era of AIDS: Anthropological and Demographic Perspectives.* Oxford: Clarendon Press, 1997.

Hulme, Peter. "Polytropic Man: Tropes of Sexuality and Mobility in Early Colonial Discourse." In *Europe and Its Others,* 2 vols., ed. Francis Barker, Peter Hulme, Margaret Iverson, and Diana Loxley, 2:17–32. Colchester: University of Essex, 1994.

Hyam, Ronald. *Empire and Sexuality: The British Experience.* Manchester: Manchester University Press, 1990.

Jensen, Kai. "Frank at Last." In *Opening the Book: New Essays on New Zealand Writers,* ed. Mark Williams and Michele Leggott, 68–82. Auckland: Auckland University Press, 1995.

Jolly, Margaret, and Lenore Manderson, eds. *Sites of Desire, Economies of Pleasure: Sexualities in Asia and the Pacific.* Chicago: University of Chicago Press, 1997.

King, Michael. *Frank Sargeson: A Life.* Auckland: Viking, 1995.

Krusenstern, Adam J. von. *Voyage round the World in the Years 1803 . . . 1806.* 2 vols. Trans. Richard Belgrave Hopper. London: John Murray, 1813.

Lamb, Jonathan. "Minute Particulars and the Representation of South Pacific Discovery." *Eighteenth-Century Studies* 28, no. 3 (1995): 281–94.

Lamb, Jonathan, Vanessa Smith, and Nicholas Thomas, eds. *Exploration and Exchange: A South Seas Anthology, 1680–1900.* Chicago: University of Chicago Press, 2000.

Lane, Christopher. *The Ruling Passion: British Colonial Rule and the Paradox of Homosexual Desire.* Durham: Duke University Press, 1995.

Langsdorff, Georg[e] H. von. *Eine Reise um die Welt.* Volume of plates. Frankfurt: Friedrich Wilmans, 1812.

——. *Voyages and Travels in Various Parts of the World, during the Years 1803 . . . 1807.* 2 vols. London: Henry Colburn, 1813.

Levy, Robert I. *Tahitians: Mind and Experience in the Society Islands.* Chicago: University of Chicago Press, 1973.

Mageo, Jeanette-Marie. "Male Transvestism and Cultural Change in Samoa." *American Ethnologist* 19, no. 3 (1992): 443–59.

——. "Samoa, on the Wilde Side: Male Transvestism, Oscar Wilde, and Liminality in Making Gender." *Ethos* 24, no. 4 (1996): 588–627.

Malinowski, Bronislaw. *A Diary in the Strict Sense of the Term.* Routledge and Kegan Paul, 1967. Reprint, intro. Raymond Firth, Stanford: Stanford University Press, 1989.

Matthews, Nancy Mowell. *Paul Gauguin: An Erotic Life.* New Haven: Yale University Press, 2001.

Maude, H. E. *Of Islands and Men: Studies in Pacific History.* Melbourne: Oxford University Press, 1968.

McClintock, Anne. *Imperial Leather: Race, Gender, and Sexuality in the Colonial Contest.* New York: Routledge, 1995.

McCormick, E. H. *Omai: Pacific Envoy.* Auckland: Auckland University Press, 1977.

Melville, Herman. *Moby Dick.* Vol. 6, *The Writings of Herman Melville.* Ed. Harrison Hayford, Hershel Parker, and G. Thomas Tanselle. Evanston: Northwestern University Press and the Newberry Library, 1988.

——. *Typee: A Peep at Polynesian Life.* Vol. 1, *The Writings of Herman Melville.* Ed. Harrison Hayford, Hershel Parker, and G. Thomas Tanselle. Evanston: Northwestern University Press and the Newberry Library, 1968.

——. *White-Jacket.* Vol. 5, *The Writings of Herman Melville.* Ed. Harrison Hayford, Hershel Parker, and G. Thomas Tanselle. Evanston: Northwestern University Press and the Newberry Library, 1970.

Miller, D. A. "Body *Bildung* and Textual Liberation." In *A New History of French Literature,* ed. Dennis Hollier, 681–87. Cambridge: Harvard University Press, 1989.

Morris, Robert J. "*Aikāne:* Accounts of Hawaiian Same-Sex Relationships in the Journals of Captain Cook's Third Voyage (1776–80)." *Journal of Homosexuality* 19 (1990): 21–54.

——. "Same-Sex Friendships in Hawaiian Lore: Constructing the Canon." In *Oceanic Homosexualities,* ed. Stephen O. Murray, 71–102. New York: Garland, 1992.

Mosse, George. *Nationalism and Sexuality.* Madison: University of Wisconsin Press, 1985.

Murray, Stephen O., ed. *Oceanic Homosexualities.* New York: Garland, 1992.

Mutiny on the Bounty. Dir. Frank Lloyd. Metro-Goldwyn-Mayer, 1935.

Mutiny on the Bounty. Dir. Lewis Milestone. Metro-Goldwyn-Mayer, 1962.

New Zealand AIDS Foundation. *Needs Assessment: Pacific Islands Men Who Have Sex with Men.* Report to North Health. November, 1996.

Obeyesekere, Gananath. *The Apotheosis of Captain Cook: European Myth-making in the Pacific.* Princeton: Princeton University Press, 1992.

——. "'British Cannibals': Contemplation of an Event in the Death and Resurrection of James Cook, Explorer." *Critical Inquiry* 18 (1992): 630–54.

O'Brian, Patrick. *Joseph Banks: A Life.* London: Collins Harvill, 1987.

Pearson, Bill. "Beginnings and Endings." *Sport* 5 (1990): 3–21.

——. *Rifled Sanctuaries: Some Views of the Pacific Islands in Western Literature to 1900.* Auckland: Auckland University Press, 1984.

Pierre et Gilles. Exhibition catalog, intro. Jonathan Turner. Sydney: Bloxham and Chambers, 1995.

Pollock, Griselda. *Avant-Garde Gambits, 1888–1893: Gender and the Colour of Art History.* London: Thames and Hudson, 1992.

Porter, Dennis. *Haunted Journeys: Desire and Transgression in European Travel Writing.* Princeton: Princeton University Press, 1991.

Pratt, Mary Louise. *Imperial Eyes: Travel Writing and Transculturation.* London: Routledge, 1992.

Prosser, Jay. *Second Skins: The Body Narratives of Transsexuality.* New York: Columbia University Press, 1998.

Ramsden, Eric. *Marsden and the Missions: Prelude to Waitangi.* Sydney: Angus and Robertson, 1936.

Rodger, N. A. M., ed. *Articles of War: The Statutes Which Governed Our Fighting Navies, 1661, 1749, and 1886.* Homewell, Hampshire: Kenneth Mason, 1982.

Rutter, Owen, ed. *The Log of the Bounty.* 2 vols. London: Golden Cockerel Press, 1937.

Sahlins, Marshall. *Historical Metaphors and Mythical Realities: Structure in the Early History of the Sandwich Islands Kingdom.* Ann Arbor: University of Michigan Press, 1981.

——. *How "Natives" Think: About Captain Cook, for Example.* Chicago: University of Chicago Press, 1995.

——. *Islands of History.* Chicago: University of Chicago Press, 1985.

Said, Edward. *Orientalism: Western Representations of the Orient.* London: Routledge, 1978.

Samwell, David. *Some Account of a Voyage to South Seas in 1776–1777–1778.* In *The Voyage of the Resolution and Discovery, 1776–1780.* Vol. 3, *The Journals of Captain James Cook on His Voyages of Discovery.* Ed. J. C. Beaglehole. London: Cambridge University Press for the Hakluyt Society, 1967.

Saper, Craig. "A Nervous Theory: The Troubling Gaze of Psychoanalysis in Media Studies." *Diacritics* 21, no. 4 (1991): 33–52.

Sargeson, Frank. Review of *An Account of New Zealand and of the Formation and Progress of the Church Missionary Society's Mission in the Northern Island*, by William Yate. *Landfall* 25, no. 3 (1971): 299–304.

Sedgwick, Eve Kosofsky. *Between Men: English Literature and Male Homosocial Desire*. New York: Columbia University Press, 1985.

———. *Epistemology of the Closet*. Berkeley: University of California Press, 1990.

———. "Nationalisms and Sexualities in the Age of Wilde." In *Nationalisms and Sexualities*, ed. Andrew Parker, Mary Russo, Doris Sommer, and Patricia Yaeger, 235–45. New York: Routledge, 1992.

Shore, Bradd. "Sexuality and Gender in Samoa: Conceptions and Misconceptions." In *Sexual Meanings: The Cultural Construction of Gender and Sexuality*, ed. Sherry B. Ortner and Harriet Whitehead, 192–215. Cambridge: Cambridge University Press, 1981.

Smith, Bernard. *European Vision and the South Pacific, 1768–1850*. Oxford: Oxford University Press, 1960.

———. *Imagining the Pacific: In the Wake of Cook's Voyages*. Melbourne: Melbourne University Press, 1992.

Smith, Vanessa. *Literary Culture and the Pacific: Nineteenth-Century Textual Encounters*. Cambridge: Cambridge University Press, 1998.

Smithyman, Kendrick. Review of *An Account of New Zealand and of the Formation and Progress of the Church Missionary Society's Mission in the Northern Island*, by William Yate. *Journal of the Polynesian Society* 82, no. 4 (1973): 434–38.

Solomon-Godeau, Abigail. "Going Native." *Art in America* 77, no. 7 (1989): 118–29, 161.

Stoler, Ann Laura. *Race and the Education of Desire: Foucault's* History of Sexuality *and the Colonial Order of Things*. Durham: Duke University Press, 1995.

Terrell, Jennifer. "Joseph Kabris and His Notes on the Marquesas." *Journal of Pacific History* 17 (1982): 101–12.

Thomas, Nicholas. *Marquesan Societies: Inequality and Political Transformation in Eastern Polynesia*. Oxford: Clarendon Press, 1990.

Thomas, Nicholas, and Diane Losche, eds. *Double Vision: Art Histories and Colonial Histories in the Pacific*. Cambridge: Cambridge University Press, 1999.

Wadley, Nicholas. Introduction to *Noa Noa: Gauguin's Tahiti*. Oxford: Phaidon, 1985.

Wannan, Bill. *Very Strange Tales: The Turbulent Times of Samuel Marsden*. Melbourne: Lansdowne Press, 1962.

Warner, Michael. "New English Sodom." *American Literature* 64, no. 1 (1992): 19–47.

Wilson, James. *A Missionary Voyage to the Southern Pacific Ocean . . . in the Ship Duff*. London: T. Chapman, 1799.

Witherington, Paul. "The Art of Melville's *Typee*." *Arizona Quarterly* 26 (1970): 136–50.

Worth, Heather. "Up on K Road on a Saturday Night: Sex, Gender, and Sex Work in Auckland." *Venereology: The Interdisciplinary, International Journal of Sexual Health* 13, no. 1 (2000): 15–24.

Yate, William. *An Account of New Zealand and of the Formation and Progress of the Church Missionary Society's Mission in the Northern Island.* 2d ed., 1835. Reprint, intro. Judith Binney, Wellington: A. H. and A. W. Reed, 1970.

Index